# larpers and shroomers

the language report

# larpers and shroomers

## the language report

### SUSIE DENT

OXFORD
UNIVERSITY PRESS

# OXFORD
UNIVERSITY PRESS

Great Clarendon Street, Oxford OX2 6DP

Oxford University Press is a department of the University of Oxford.
It furthers the University's objective of excellence in research, scholarship,
and education by publishing worldwide in

Oxford New York

Auckland Bangkok Buenos Aires Cape Town
Chennai Dar es Salaam Delhi Hong Kong Istanbul Karachi
Kolkata Kuala Lumpur Madrid Melbourne Mexico City Mumbai Nairobi
São Paulo Shanghai Taipei Tokyo Toronto

Oxford is a registered trade mark of Oxford University Press
in the UK and in certain other countries

Published in the United States
by Oxford University Press Inc., New York

British Library Cataloguing in Publication Data
Data available

Library of Congress Cataloging in Publication Data
Data available

ISBN 0–19–861012-2

1

Typeset in Miller and Meta
by Paul Saunders
Printed in Great Britain by
Clays Ltd, St Ives plc.

# Contents

# Acknowledgements

Despite the single name on the title page, *larpers and shroomers* is very much a team effort. The book is informed throughout by the evidence of Oxford's extensive language-monitoring programme, which collects over 200,000 quotations a year charting language and vocabulary change. The correct interpretation of this evidence, which was skillfully filtered by James McCracken, is an expert task, and Catherine Soanes and Angus Stevenson were both enormous allies in compiling the final selections for the book—a near impossible (and far less fun) task without them. Andrew Ball, Bill Trumble, Jane McCauley, and Penny Silva all provided vital material from the *Oxford English Dictionary*, together with personal insight and interpretation. Jenni Scott, a seasoned blogger, helped greatly on the section dealing with language online, while the BBC's Catherine Sangster contributed much of the material on our changing pronunciation.

The study of developments in World English vocabulary owes a lot to many of OUP's expert advisers from around the world. Bruce Moore, Desmond Hurley, Tony Deverson, Leela Pienaar, Jennifer Eagleton, Katherine Barber, Satarupa Chaudhuri, and Fadilah Jasmani all provided material documenting English's evolution in their respective countries.

Orin Hargraves is to be thanked for many of the colourful instances of language change in the US, and Erin McKean once again offered humour and wisdom throughout the book's compilation. In the UK, my commissioning editor Judy Pearsall's expertise was crucial, as was her support, and Rachel De Wachter, Nick Clarke, and Carol Alexander all skilfully managed a fairly hair-raising schedule. Julia Elliott's copy-editing was as enlightening as essential, and John Taylor's cartoons, as always, produced smiles from all. The excellent websites of Paul McFedries (*www.wordspy.com*) and Michael Quinion (*www.worldwidewords.com*) are endlessly browsable as well as a source of inspiration.

Finally, thanks are due to two people in particular. Richard Digance proved a fount of knowledge on subjects as varied as slang and cricket; his light-hearted touch was always welcome. Elizabeth Knowles proved the very best of advisers: beyond her unstinting encouragement, her knowledge on almost every subject I sent her way never failed to astound. Many of the book's most colourful examples are due to her.

### Note on trademarks and proprietary status

This book includes some words which have, or are asserted to have, proprietary status as trademarks or otherwise. Their inclusion does not imply that they have acquired for legal purposes a non-proprietary or general significance, nor any other judgement concerning their legal status.

# Introduction

**Language tethers us to the world; without it we spin like atoms.**
British novelist Penelope Lively in *Moon Tiger*, 1987.

A poll carried out in 2004 by the Plain English Campaign produced a league table of the clichés most detested by the English-speaking world. Top place went to *at the end of the day*, followed closely by *at this moment in time*. The combined picture of these and a host of other sources of irritation was seen by some to offer up a picture of the language at its most wrung out: a perfect distillation of its decline. Together with the ubiquitous use of 'fillers' such as *like* and *totally*, the vast lexicon of English is said to have shrunk to a bland collection of age-worn phrases.

If this is rather an extreme account of the fears of some, there are certainly many people today who long for the linguistic equivalent of 'firm government', a return to a past when grammatical rules were learned and adhered to, and words meant what they were supposed to mean. For them, and in that golden age, vocabulary was also infinitely richer. The language changes charted in *larpers and shroomers* suggest a very different picture. Developments in slang, new turns of idiomatic and euphemistic phrase, and colourful creations in contexts as varied as business and sport all reflect the undiminished momentum of a language which, far from looking backwards, continues to evolve at a strikingly fast pace. Moreover, the selection of new terms in the pages that follow represents only a tiny fraction of the new coinages being made.

A report on language as it stands at a particular moment provides a chance to catch many items which may not endure, and which consequently may never make it into a printed dictionary. Before the Internet and the conversational worlds of emails, chat rooms, and weblogs, many such words would never have left their initial environments. Now they can take off within days. These virtual words are also creating new lexicons to serve their own members, be they *bloggers, lurkers, larpers,* or *leets* (see pages 61–67). Such cyberslang is one of the most productive—and colourful—areas of new-word coining today.

New words are far more about reinvention than we may think. As few as one per cent of those recorded in the *Oxford English Dictionary* are created entirely from scratch. Of the 900 included on average for every year of the twentieth century, that leaves 891 which result from the adaptation of the old: the mixing of existing words, the blending of parts of words, or simply old words put to new uses as their shifting environment requires. Far from suggesting a language turned in on itself, the new words emerging from these processes can be as dramatic as any entirely new creation. Particularly colourful are the results of playful mixing: *buttlegging, coinkydoinkys,* and *binikis* (pages 23, 72, and 48 respectively) are just three of the hundreds of clever and apposite reincarnations enjoying currency today.

This circularity of vocabulary can result in fascinating individual word histories, which show how older words survive through adaptation. (So a *deer* once meant any animal, and *meat* any food: they became more specific when we needed them to.) As a result, *larpers and shroomers* is as much about history's influence on language as about the influence exerted by contemporary events and preoccupations. History is helpful in other respects too. A list of modern euphemisms shows a concentration on terms related to drugs, ethnicity, and redundancy—compare this to the subjects requiring linguistic soft focus a century ago, notably childbirth, mental illness, and prostitution, and we gain considerable insight into modern concerns. Similarly, the realization that many of today's strongly taboo words were perfectly acceptable centuries ago throws up intriguing questions as to our changing tastes and sensibilities. By contrast, a comparison of newspaper headlines from 1904 with those of today reveals unexpected similarities in the coverage of death and crime, even as the differences between the puns so beloved of today's tabloids and the deadpan leaders of newspapers from a century ago fairly shout out from the page.

◈

2004 saw some examples of highly specific vocabulary cropping up in surprising places. The Deputy Chief Constable of North Wales, Clive Wolvendale, amused many and angered others by performing rap at the inaugural meeting of his local Black Police Association (*I'm just a white boy called the Deputy CC. They said I'd never make it as a bitchin' MC*), while Pentagon- and Downing Street- controlled politics was turned into cabaret in the British play *Follow My Leader*, which included song and dance numbers about *pre-emptive defence*. Both situations showed the hijacking of very contextualized vocabularies; by contrast, the language of television is almost predetermined to spread, and quickly. The series *Friends*, which came to an end in 2004, was said to have influenced the language of an entire generation (according to one academic, its crowning achievement was the spread of the filler *so*, as in *it's so over*). Programmes such as *Little Britain* (and its signature teen phrase *yeah but no but yeah but*) and the Australian *Kath and Kim* with its endless word play (*foxymorons, clutching at spanners*) look likely to take over as sources of successful catchphrases and idioms.

◈

2004 was the year in which pedantry became cool. The phenomenal success throughout the English-speaking world of Lynne Truss's *Eats, Shoots and Leaves* made punctuation and its abuse an unexpected talking point, and one arousing some passion. Truss was quickly heralded as the champion of rules, and her book praised as a backlash against a descriptive (rather than prescriptive) approach to language change. Such has been its success that the name of the book itself has become an idiom to be played upon. *Jordan scores, eats Truss and arrives* announced an article in the *Sunday Times*, detailing the autobiography of the model-turned-celebrity Jordan and its accounts of her relationships with footballers—the book knocked Lynne Truss off the British best-seller charts.

◈

The first *language report*, published in 2003, inevitably contained much about the vocabulary of war. While the headlines of 2004 continued to be dominated by the ongoing conflict in Iraq, many of the defining terms of the war—*embeds, mouseholing, decapitation exercise*—gave way to more figurative language. The image of the *fog of war*, a term coined by the Prussian military thinker Karl von Clausewitz, cropped up frequently in debates over whether the military action in Iraq was, indeed, *just*. Meanwhile, the phrase *thin red line*, used by the British military in the late nineteenth century to describe the scarlet-uniformed armies of Queen Victoria, was also resurrected to describe a line in the sand in both Iraq and the Middle East, the overstepping of which would demand a *rapid response*. Such martial metaphors stood alongside others less solemn, and occasionally of the mixed variety, including George W. Bush's protest that Senator John McCain *can't take the high horse and claim the low road.*

In all of these areas, *larpers and shroomers* can cover only a fraction of the colourful changes in English that have emerged over the past twelve months. Many of them may already have been overtaken. Whatever their chances of survival, each new development is proof that, far from being wrung out, our language is as robust and versatile as ever. It may not change as we would like it to, but few of us would want it to stand still in the face of our rapidly changing environment.

Susie Dent, 2004

# Bubbling Under:
## The Words of the Moment

Dictionaries are but the depositories of words already legitimated by usage.
Society is the work-shop in which new ones are elaborated.

Thomas Jefferson, American politician, statesman, and writer.

For last year's words belong to last year's language
And next year's words await another voice.

T. S. Eliot, *Four Quartets*, 1944.

Most old bums start out as young bums. They cut school, they hung out . . . until
one day they were gray-headed, no teeth in their mouth, and the young guy that
everybody thought was cool was just an old bum on his way to old bumblehood.
That's a new word. Trust me. Write that down.

Al Sharpton, American clergyman and civil rights activist, writing in *The Weekly Standard*,
23 February 2004.

The criteria for including a new word in a dictionary are stringent.
Tempting as it is to add new words as soon as they appear, any neologism
(a new coinage) needs first to have shown clear signs of semi-permanence
and of fairly wide usage. As a very rough rule applied by Oxford's
contemporary lexicographers, a word must be cited at least five times, over
five years, and by five independent sources in the databases of the Oxford
Reading Programme (which itself collects over 200,000 citations a year in
its continuous task of tracking the English language) in order to justify
inclusion in one of the major dictionaries of the English language.

The records of the *Oxford English Dictionary* are vast, but the number of neologisms coined at any one time will always exceed those represented in its pages. Equally, no dictionary of current English can hope to do justice to the creativity of English users, for whom language is an endlessly versatile tool. We are consciously playing with and on our vocabularies every day, even if the vast majority of the results remain the inventions of a moment. Thanks to the unprecedented number and variety of media available to us, a new word can spread, quite literally, overnight, whereupon it may enjoy a few weeks of headlines before disappearing either to the very fringes of vocabulary or to obscurity altogether. By taking a snapshot of the language at a single moment in time, we can catch some of those words which enjoy only the briefest of stays in the lexical limelight.

The following list attempts to do some justice to words which are, like releases in the singles charts, 'bubbling under', and which are under scrutiny from dictionary-makers looking for signs of survival. Only a percentage will ever achieve permanence in a dictionary. Without them, however, and irrespective of their future, a view of the world as it is experienced now would be incomplete.

## Some fizzlers

Many words, in spite of their colour, have never (yet?) achieved inclusion in an English dictionary. For example:

**sylvanshine:** the shine given off at night by certain trees and shrubs when light reflects off drops of dew. The term was coined by the US professor of meteorology Alastair B. Fraser in 1994.

**fizzgiggious:** one of many nonsense words coined by Edward Lear, this one describing a *fizzgiggious fish* who walks on stilts because he has no legs.

**rememble:** a false memory, especially of some place, event, or object of one's childhood. Also used as a verb: *I remembled the house as being bigger*. Coined by Elan Cole on the US radio show *The Next Big Thing*.

**flirr:** a photograph that features the camera operator's finger in the corner. This is one of many 'sniglets' ('Any Word That Doesn't Appear in the Dictionary but Should') coined by US comedian Rich Hall.

**inoculatte:** to take coffee 'intravenously' when you are running late: the verb was a runner-up in the 2002 Washington Post Style Invitational for new words.

Unlike the above, the following words are likely to find their way into the printed record of English (indeed some already have been included in the *Concise Oxford English Dictionary*). The key criterion will always be frequency: once there is sufficient evidence of wider usage, so the need for a definition in the public domain increases.

# phishing

**phishing** (a respelling of *fishing*): the fraudulent practice of luring visitors to plausible but fake websites and persuading them to enter their credit card details.

# bluejacking

**bluejacking:** the sending of (often mischievous) text messages to strangers whose mobile phone numbers have been picked up by Bluetooth devices, capable of 'talking' to another device within a range of a few metres. The word is a blend of *Bluetooth* and *hijacking*.

# toothing

**toothing:** the use of a Bluetooth-enabled mobile phone to arrange sexual encounters. Having discovered a phone in the same area (as in 'bluejacking' above), the question **toothing?** is usually sent as an initial greeting.

# conspicuous compassion

**conspicuous compassion:** the ostentatious expression of sympathy over high-profile deaths in order to look good, rather than for any more sincere motive. The phrase is a successor to **recreational grief**, and sits alongside other terms (listed by Patrick West in a report by the

British think tank Civitas) such as **grief-lite**, and **mourning sickness**. The nation has replaced the social ties of church and family with the rites of conspicuous compassion—the piling up of rotting flowers and sodden teddy bears, the 'lapel loutism' of empathy ribbons and the staging of ever-lengthening minutes of silence.

*The Telegraph*, Calcutta, February 2004, quoting from the Civitas press release.

# LARPing

**LARPing** (= 'Live Action Role Playing'): the hobby of re-enacting fantasy scenarios by dressing up and assuming character roles. Participants are known as **LARPers**.

LARPing fires the imagination. It's like playing 'let's pretend' when you're a kid. We've simply chosen not to grow out of that. And now we've got better toys.

Journalist and LARPer Ed Fortune, quoted in *The Guardian*, December 2003.

# chugger

**chugger** (a blend of *charity mugger*): charity fund-raisers who stop people in the street in the hope of signing them up to their cause. The act of doing so is known as **chugging**.

# sexile

**sexile:** to force your college room-mate to go elsewhere when you wish to 'entertain' a guest. This US term is also used as a noun, and those excluded are known as **sexiles**.

I was one of the lucky ones. Yes, I shared a room during my first year, with an athletics student from Cincinatti called Caci. But, whatever our differences, neither would dream of sexiling the other.

Gabriella Windsor, writing in the *Sunday Times*, February 2004.

# testosteronic

**testosteronic:** highly macho, in a stereotypical way.

And at least Thelma and Louise stop short of emulating Butch Cassidy and the Sundance Kid, who use their remaining ammunition to go out in a blaze of testosteronic glory.

Margaret Carlson, *Anyone Can Grow Up: How George Bush and I Made It to the White House*, May 2003.

# superspreader

**superspreader:** a person with a 'high viral load' (the quantity of viruses present in a given volume of blood) and who is also highly infectious. In

2003 the similar term **superinfector**, with all its deliberate echoes of **superbug**, achieved high prominence in the wake of the SARS virus. That means identifying potential superspreaders is vital to halting SARS—except that scientists don't know what makes a superspreader super.

*Time* magazine, April 2003.

# choice fatigue

**choice fatigue:** a condition suffered by consumers who are offered too much choice. According to the US psychologist Barry Schwartz, there are two consumer types: **maximizers**, who always relentlessly seek out the best, and **satisficers**, who stop searching as soon as they find something that adequately fulfils their needs.

# threequel

**threequel:** a sequel to a sequel, usually used in reference to films. The cutting out of . . . both the educational slant of the first [Jurassic Park] and the excesses of the second makes for a leaner, if less surprising, dino threequel.

*Total Film*, March 2002.

# blondespeak

**blondespeak:** a tongue-in-cheek term for language simple enough for dizzy blondes to understand. A moment of silliness is also referred to as a **blonde moment**.

# retrosexual

**retrosexual:** a man who spends as little time and money as possible on his appearance. The term is the opposite of the term **metrosexual** (a fashion-conscious heterosexual male), voted by the American Dialect Society as the word of 2003.

Metrosexuals are scrupulous about their grooming and are great consumers of men's cosmetic products. They use hair gel. Retrosexuals are scared of hair gel.

Margaret Wente in *The Globe and Mail* (Canada), February 2004.

# Google bombing

**Google bombing:** the manipulation of Google's search-engine results, usually for political or mischievous ends.

George W. Bush has been Google bombed. Web users entering the words 'miserable failure' into the popular search engine are directed to the biography of the president on the White House website.

*BBCi News*, December 2003.

# gangmaster

**gangmaster:** someone who employs 'gangs' of casual labourers to supply local agriculture and industry. There is no surviving legal definition of the term, but the first citation for it in the *Oxford English Dictionary* is from 1884 (*His young children . . . taken from him and put under the care of a gangmaster*). It became a high-profile term following the death of Chinese cockle-pickers in Morecambe, England, in February 2004.

Weak voluntary codes offer no protection from illegal hours, low pay or intimidation, and the authorities do not have the means to keep track of gangmasters' activities.

Labour MP Jim Sheridan, February 2004.

# laughter club

**laughter club:** a phenomenon in parts of India in which groups of people gather to laugh loudly in public with the aim of relieving stress.

The standard routine at a laughter club begins with some deep-breathing exercises, then a group chant in unison, 'Ho-Ho-Ha-Ha-Ho-Ho-Ha-Ha . . .'. . . Next, members run through a medley of seven different types of laughs (including the hearty laugh, dancing laugh, swinging laugh and cocktail laugh).

Canadian writer Michael Kerr on his website.

# freeganism

**freeganism:** a philosophy which promotes obtaining as much of one's food as possible from free sources, such as food thrown away by restaurants. The movement started out as an offshoot of veganism, and the term itself is a blend of *free* and *veganism*. It is also used as an example of **voluntary simplicity**, encompassing a broad philosophy of 'ethical eating'.

Remember in an episode of Seinfeld, where George Costanza goes for that eclaire [*sic*] that is sitting in the trash? That's freeganism.

James McQuiston, *www.neufutur.com*.

# stage-phoning

**stage-phoning:** talking on a mobile phone in an animated, and deliberately audible, manner. The phrase was coined by British researcher Sadie Plant in a report written for the mobile phone company Motorola, and has since been taken up more widely.

# DWY

**DWY** (= driving while yakking): driving while speaking on a cellphone. This US abbreviation is a play on the legal term *DWI*, 'driving while impaired', and is one of many such combinations, including *DWB* ('driving while black', referring to the alleged habit of police of stopping black drivers for no reason).

# latte factor

**latte factor:** a term coined by David Bach, author of *The Automatic Millionaire*, and now more widely used by economists to describe the apparently insignificant daily purchases which can add up to significant expenditure over time.

David Bach says you don't need a lot of time or money to make a million dollars. If you save five dollars a day, you'll be a millionaire in 41 years. David says you'll find the money in what he calls your 'latte factor,' the money you spend everyday on things like fancy drinks and eating out.

*www.oprah.com*

# flash mob

**flash mob:** a group of complete strangers who gather in a public place at an arranged time (organized via the Net or texting) to perform a pointless act before dispersing.

At precisely 6.31 yesterday evening, Sofas UK in central London found itself at the cutting edge of Internet culture. Simultaneously, and not coincidentally, it was also besieged by 250 sweaty people speaking English without the letter 'o'. Sofas UK was the chosen venue for Britain's first 'flash mob'.

*The Guardian*, August 2003.

# bookcrossing

**bookcrossing:** the sharing of a book that one has enjoyed by leaving it in a public place to be picked up and read by random passers-by. Participants use a special website to register the book, add their comments on it, and identify it with a unique ID number. They then leave the book in a public place such as a shop or train for anyone to pick up. The person who finds it can trace the history of the book via the website, add their own comments on it, and then again leave the book 'in the wild' for another reader to find.

# Ctrl-Alt-Delete

**Ctrl-Alt-Delete:** a mechanism which allows you to force a computer to quit. A metaphorical use of the common computing key combination is also known as the **three-fingered salute**.

It's time to hit Ctrl-Alt-Delete on the computerized Bowl Championship Series. Or should we now call it the Bowl Split-Championship Series?

David Thomas in the *Fort Worth Star Telegram*, December 2003.

# movieoke

**movieoke:** a form of entertainment, based on karaoke, in which a person acts out scenes from a film while a silent version of it plays in the background.

The opportunity to mouth 'You talkin' to me?' from *Taxi Driver* and 'Go ahead, punk, make my day' from *Dirty Harry* has long been irresistible. The surprise is that movieoke, a twist on the karaoke sing-along craze, has only just arrived.

*www.news.com.au*, February 2004.

# microscission

**microscission:** a new way of delivering drugs to the body without the need for injections, in which a blast of gas opens up tiny passages in the skin through which medicine can be transmitted. The technique is a boon to those who suffer from **aichmophobia** (a fear of needles), and **tyranophobia** (a fear of injections).

# Googlewhacking

**Googlewhacking:** the game of entering a two-word search into the Google search engine and trying to get just a single 'hit' in return. Recent Googlewhacks (the single-page results) include *musclebound okapi* and *codswallop usurps*. The Google part of Googlewhacking is self-explanatory, while the second element is probably a pun on 'whack' (to strike something forcefully, or a forceful hit) and 'whack off', a slang phrase meaning 'masturbate'. The term might also hark back to the term *bushwhack*, describing an engagement in warfare, prominent during the 2003 conflict in Iraq and used to more ironic effect in 2004 in references to George W. Bush.

# skier

**skier:** a person of the so-called 'golden generation' who spends their savings to enjoy their retirement to the full. The term is based on the acronym for 'spend kids' inheritance'.

# guerrilla gig:

**guerrilla gig:** a performance by a band in an unlikely venue, where they play until they are evicted. Details of the gig are communicated by word of mouth, websites, and text messaging among fans.

## Dord: the infamous 'ghost word'

Dictionary-makers do, very occasionally, make mistakes. One of the most famous errors of the twentieth century was the appearance of the word **dord**, which appeared in the second edition of *Webster's New International Dictionary* in 1934. The term was listed, on page 771, as a noun meaning density in the fields of physics and chemistry, and there it remained for five years before the error was spotted. The mistake was due to the erroneous filing of an index card (then the preferred system of collecting words) for the abbreviation '**D or d**', indicating density. As Philip Babcock Gove, editor-in-chief of the third edition of *Webster's New International Dictionary*, wrote in a 1954 article: 'As soon as someone else entered the pronunciation, dord was given the slap on the back that sent breath into its being'. While the word has now sadly been removed from Webster's dictionary, it continued to reappear for several years afterwards in other dictionaries which used Webster's as a source.

# 2

# Words Apart:
# 1904 VS 2004

**Our language, or any civilised language, is like the phoenix: it springs anew from its own ashes.**
T. S. Eliot, quoted in L. Michaels and C. Ricks, *The State of the Language*, 1980.

To compare the vocabulary of two decades, a century apart, is to reveal two apparently contradictory characteristics of language change. A search through the *Oxford English Dictionary* (*OED*) for the new words of 1904 produces a striking number of terms which have a very recent feel, thanks to their continuing resonance today: *backtracking*, *hip* (well informed), *wiretapping*, *newsflash*, and *scandal sheets* are all, startlingly, first documented one hundred years ago. The same search, however, reveals another vocabulary which bears the unmistakable stamp of its period, including words whose usefulness came to an end as circumstances changed. *Pip pip* was coined in 1904 to imitate the sound of a car horn and proved the predecessor of *toodle-pip* and *toodle-oo* in the 1920s, while the *hippomobile*, a horse-drawn vehicle taking its name from the Greek *hippos*, 'horse', was gone by the end of the decade.

The opening years of the twentieth century were ones of great change, and language necessarily kept pace. The 1900s saw the expansion of media such as newspapers, mass-market comic strips, film, cartoons, and radio, as well as major advances in the fields of psychology and transportation. In these last two categories, the terms *empathy*, *Everywoman*, and *masochistic* were the result of the focus on the processes of the mind, while in the area of transportation, motoring was becoming a major hobby.

## The advent of the car

**Goggles are, unhappily, almost a necessity when travelling at any but the lowest speeds.**
A. B. F. Young, in *The Complete Motorist*, 1904.

**Fancy a motor car coming into the garden! It will be such a treat.**
From Rudyard Kipling's *They*, published in 1904.

1904 saw the publication, in Dublin, of possibly the first dictionary of motoring by R. J. Mecredy, a work which currently provides the first evidence in the *OED* for *brake pedal, gasket,* and *suction stroke.* In the same year, *speedometer, dashboard, parking strip* and *petrol consumption* are also first documented. On 4 May 1904, Charles Stewart Rolls and Frederick Henry Royce agreed to meet to discuss possible collaborations given their respective interests in motor cars. Out of that meeting the *Rolls Royce* was born. A hundred years later, a new (and probably less desirable) car accessory is the *alcolock*, a breathalyzing device which monitors a driver's alcohol levels.

In 1904, the continuing process of urbanization was reflected in a large number of new terms, including *megalopolitan* (relating to the way of life of a *megalopolis*, or large city), *town planning*, and *town centres*. At the same time, the various political manoeuvrings in the world began to set the stage for conflict, even as the Boer War came to an end, and the importance of weaponry and war tactics remained—*minesweeping* was a term, and a process, dating back to 1904, a year in which *dugouts* and *firing squads* were also born.

On 8 April 1904 the so-called 'Entente Cordiale' was established in a treaty between Britain and France. The Entente signalled an end to centuries of conflict which culminated in Napoleon's wars, and also heralded the world-war alliance between the two biggest European democracies against Germany. Whilst, in the centenary year of the Entente, Britons and the French are said to hold more enmity than friendship towards each other (a poll carried out for the French newspaper *Libération* and Britain's *The Guardian* suggested that the French think Britons anti-European, and that Britons regard the French as arrogant), the linguistic influences of each country are not in doubt. It is perhaps appropriate that in 1904 itself words such as *blouson*, *diamanté*, and *violette de Parme* were borrowed into English.

If the events of the twenty-first century are rather different from those a hundred years earlier, the new words of 2004 suggest that at least some of our preoccupations remain the same. A focus on war and technology is as linguistically evident in the opening decade of the last century as in the present one, and other themes such as fashion and food remain a rich source of new vocabulary. Independent of history, however, is the inventiveness characterizing many of the new coinages from both decades. Words such as *gongoozler*, *lollapalooza*, *griefer*, and *jujy* (see below) may stay rooted in their respective eras, but they are also a vivid showcase for the timeless versatility of language, and for our creativeness with it.

The following selection of words from the early years of each century hint at some of the issues—both light and serious—influencing language change.

## 1904

**lollapalooza:** something outstandingly good of its kind. The term originated as US slang and was in its early days also spelt as *lalapalooza* and *lallapalootza*.
**Saturday night we had our final parade with the fireworks finish, and it was a lallapalootza!**
> H. McHugh, *I'm from Missouri*, 1904.

**shock wave:** a disturbance that travels through a fluid as a narrow region in which there is a large and abrupt change in pressure and related quantities. The first figurative use of the term did not appear until 1969, and is now the more normal modern use.

**Randlord:** the owner or manager of a gold-field on the Rand in South Africa.
**The Randlord's proposal really drives the British workman out of the Transvaal.**
> *Daily Chronicle*, 1904.

**teletype:** to operate a teleprinter, a telegraph instrument for transmitting telegraph messages as they are typed, and for printing incoming ones.
We must teletype as well as teletalk.
*Daily News*, 1904.

**trotteur** (also known as a *trotter skirt* or *trotteuse*): a short, neat walking skirt.
Seaside dresses . . . are short, and the pleated trotteur skirt can scarcely be improved upon.
*Westminster Gazette*, 1909.

**bonzer** (Australian and New Zealand slang): excellent, extremely good. The term is possibly an alteration of *bonanza*.

**midinette:** a French, especially Parisian, shop girl or milliner's assistant. In extended use the term described a fashionable but empty-headed young girl.
The Parisian . . . is tired of the absurd hat. The midinette and those of her kind have made it impossible.
*Westminster Gazette*, 1909.

**neo-realist:** an advocate of a new or revived form of realism.
Naturally there is repellent music in the score; but then the neo-realists insist on truth, not on the pursuit of vague and decorative beauty.
J. Huneker, *Overtones*, 1904.

**gongoozler:** an idler who stares at length at activity on a canal. The term was used more widely to describe a person who stares protractedly at something.
Pronounced slowly and with the proper emphasis, 'gongoozler' merits a very high place in the vocabulary of opprobrium.
*Daily Chronicle*, 1906.

**It:** sex appeal. The term was first recorded in the works of Rudyard Kipling in 1904, but did not really take off until the 1920s, when it was the title of a romantic novel by Elinor Glyn. *It-girl* is still a popular term today, describing a woman (and socialite) who has achieved celebrity through her sex appeal.

'Tisn't beauty, so to speak, nor good talk necessarily. It's just It. Some women'll stay in a man's memory if they once walk down a street.
Rudyard Kipling, *Traffics and Discoveries*, 1904.

# 2004

**love beeper:** a small electronic device which beeps if another person with an opposite sex beeper comes within range. The device is Japanese in origin and is also known under its trademark 'lovegety'.

**darknet:** an internet underworld in which people illegally share copyrighted music files and other software. The term was first coined by a group of Microsoft employees.
The darknet! Jeez, are they trying to make piracy cool? Who'd want to hang out on the boring old Internet when the other kids are on the darknet?
Paul Boutin on *www.slate.msn.com*, 2004.

**jujy** (pronounced *juh-jee*)**:** gorgeous; stylish. The term originally comes from 'Polari', a slang used by gay communities. It is becoming increasingly popular within the fashion industry.
They have a Queer Eye for the Straight Guy (LivingTV). They are, in their own words, like, totally jujy.
*The Guardian*, 2003.

**alcolock:** a device fitted to a car's ignition which monitors the level of alcohol in a driver's breath; the car will not start if the driver is over the legal limit.

**togethering:** taking a holiday with one's extended family and friends. The term has been trademarked by a US travel marketing firm, but evidence of general use dates back to 2002.
More and more Americans are vacationing in a loving gang it seems. This trend towards mob bonding is called 'togethering'.
*San Diego Union-Tribune*, 2004.

**griefer:** a participant in a *MMORPG*, or *Massive Multi-Player Online Role-Playing Game*, who tries to disrupt the game by any means possible.
Any MMORPG that has something like perma-death will encourage the worst kind of players.

All the exploiters, macroers, griefers, cheats will be attracted to it . . . It's no fun for most people to kill computer AI stuff when you can kill another player and make them mad and ruin their gaming experience.

Post on the message board of *www.mmorpg.net*.

**SPIM** (or **spim**): unwanted advertising sent via instant messaging systems on a computer. The term is a variation on the word *spam*, meaning unsolicited email.

Spimming tools include chatroom hosts that pose as humans, persuading others to add them to their buddy list, thus exposing the victim to spim.

*www.computing.net*

**hiving:** making one's home the focus for every activity, including work, whilst actively connecting with the outside community. This new trend in modern living is seen as the opposite of *cocooning*, a term from the 1980s which described the perceived American need to retreat from the realities of the world.

Borrowing from the metaphor of a beehive, abuzz with activity, hiving represents engagement, interaction and connection with the outside environment. Although Americans have indicated increased anxiety and uncertainty about the future, they seek comfort and connection with others. And more so than ever, this is found at home.

*www.yankelovich.com*, 2004.

**retifism:** shoe fetishism. The term is derived from the name of an eighteenth-century French educator and novelist, Nicholas-Edme Rétif de la Bretonne, who chronicled in detail his own sexual fantasies.

According to William Rossi, author of the toe-curlingly funny thesis *Sex life of the foot and shoe* (Kreiger Press, 1997), podiatrists are ignorant of the sex life of feet despite the undoubted role they play in intimate interactions between humans. The subject of . . . retifism and foot fetishism is poorly understood by the scientific community and often ignored by the judiciary.

*www.podiatry.curtin.edu.au*, 2004.

**ASBO:** antisocial behaviour order. The term denotes a civil order introduced under the Crime and Disorder Act to protect the public from antisocial behaviour such as abusive language, vandalism, drunkenness, and joyriding.

# 3

# Something Borrowed, Something New

Nastylgia is the latest term for any sentiment along the lines of 'At least under Benito the trains ran on time'.
*The Observer*, November 2003.

Cheers and bunting for Banksy, 'nom-de-spray' of the graffiti artist who bypassed the usual approach to exhibiting at Tate Britain by . . . sticking his picture up himself.
*The Independent*, October 2003.

Men also devolve into 'groomzillas', sometimes asserting their authority over details considered the bride's domain, such as flowers and even her gown.
*Ladies Home Journal*, 2003, demonstrating the linguistic transition from 'bridezilla' (an overzealous bride who changes for the worse in the run-up to the wedding) to 'groomzilla'.

The press treatment of the 'lippygate' photographs of Cherie Blair and Carole Caplin on the Blairs' marital bed in Downing Street is a further example of the changing attitude to the Prime Minister.
*Daily Telegraph*, August 2003.

How do new words come about? Most of us think of them as the invention of a moment, the colourful and romantic inspiration of a single person. In fact, only around one per cent of all new words in English today are completely new, and of those an even smaller percentage are conjured up out of thin air. The vast majority of neologisms are the result of a variety of different processes directing the evolution of language. They are no less striking, and certainly no less significant, because of it. All new words, whatever their origin, are what the American writer Cullen Murphy once described as 'the birth certificates of change'.

## Mixing and matching

Of the various mechanisms by which new words are established, probably the most productive is the combination of existing words, or parts of words. The versatility of our language makes the number of possible combinations infinite, although each period will have its own favourite starting points. Popular pairings of the twenty-first century include various combinations of -*chic*, and -*wash*, the use of modifiers and prefixes such as *spinach* and *Franken-*, and a host of versions of things -*lite*. Interestingly, many of the original ideas behind words such as 'Franken-' (Frankenstein having created a monster) and 'spinach' (being good for you) are much older than their modern developments.

## -chic:

**-chic:** denoting a fashion or style.

council chic

lounge-biker chic

shabby chic

prairie chic

chip-shop chic

## -wash:

**-wash:** denoting a deliberate attempt to change the appearance of something (modelled on the term 'whitewash').

blackwash (to bring information out of concealment; to disclose).

bluewash (an attempt to grant retrospective legitimacy to an illegal occupation).

greenwash (to give out disinformation so as to present an environmentally responsible public image).

gold wash (more than a whitewash, 'like spraying a dungheap with gold', according to the *Toronto Globe and Mail*).

# Expanding contractions

The enormous influence upon informal language of texting, chat rooms, and email, all of which call for a concision of vocabulary and effort, has accelerated an age-old mechanism for creating new words: the use of abbreviations and acronyms. The forms born in these contexts are also starting to influence more formal language—business jargon, for example, already boasts a large number of acronyms such as **B2B** (business to business)—while the vocabulary of computing is full of abbreviations and initialisms which to the uninitiated are as baffling as the technologies themselves, including **DSL** (digital subscriber line), **P2P** (peer to peer), and **IMing** (instant messaging over the Internet).

Abbreviated forms can eventually become as commonplace as the terms for which they are shorthand: occurrences of **WMD** in 2004, for example, were rapidly catching up with the full term 'weapons of mass destruction'. Other abbreviations—such as the colourful **romzomcom** for 'romantic zombie comedy', which extends the more established 'romcom' and has been used almost exclusively in reference to the film *Shaun of the Dead*—are the creations of a specific moment and may not stay around for long.

# Words on loan

By far the majority of words used in English today are of foreign origin, be it Latin or Greek or, more recently, from almost all the languages in Europe and beyond. This does not include the many thousands of words absorbed into British and American English from other national varieties of English worldwide.

Most 'loanwords' are appropriated because of cultural influences—food and drink, health remedies and therapies, science and horticulture, are all areas in which English is borrowing readily from other languages. **Ostalgie**, a nostalgia for East Germany pre-1989, was a term much discussed in the wake of the film *Goodbye Lenin* and has been readily absorbed into English in the 2000s, as have **budo** (from Japanese, meaning 'martial arts'), and **glatt** (from Yiddish, meaning 'completely kosher').

## The survival of the fittest

How many new words are created by means of the processes above? The *Oxford English Dictionary* records approximately 90,000 new words over the course of the twentieth century, meaning, very roughly, 900 new words or changes in meaning in every year. Such a number represents only a tiny minority of the thousands of new words appearing in English each year; most will disappear before they achieve semi-permanence in a dictionary. Such a low survival rate does not, however, diminish their significance.

There are a handful of primary factors which determine the survival of a new word, of which the most important are probably usefulness, user-friendliness, and, crucially, exposure. Without the latter, the guarantee of usage, a new word will not survive. 'Custom', wrote Ben Jonson in 1640, 'is the most certain mistress of language, as the public stamp makes the current money.'

# 4

# Talking on the Level:
## Biz Words and Buzz Words

The language of the workplace is often polarized between the top and bottom levels of employee—between the metaphors of management-speak and the coded slang of the workforce, designed to be impenetrable to all but those on the shop floor. Today's business lexicon, much of which is of US origin, continues to invite this rather crude analysis, by offering up numerous examples of colourful jargon and covert rebellion.

Terminology on the commercial shop floor is often subversive—words seen by employees as being the most objectionable examples of management rhetoric are converted into forms which mock their original. Alan Chapman, an expert in organizational development, runs a website (*www.businessballs.com*) listing hundreds of business terms employed by senior management, as well as the less generous alternatives offered by their subordinates. While Chapman defends such acronyms as **AIDA** ('attention, interest, desire, action': the responses to effective advertising) as useful strategic tools, he also acknowledges rather more alternative examples such as **FEAR** ('forget everything and run'), **BANJO** ('bang another nuisance job out'), and **FORD** ('found on roadside, dead', used to describe a project which has virtually no chance of success).

Far from being the result of bland 'jargonics', many new business terms are highly colourful and employ figurative language to powerful effect. Idioms such as **putting skin in the game** (making a financial commitment to a company in which one is interested) and **dropping your pants** (lowering the price of a product in order to close a sale) suggest a commercial spirit of adventure and humour, while the striking images of a **cockroach problem** and **leg-lifting** belie the rather more prosaic processes they describe (respectively, a problem that is bigger than it initially appears, and the selling of one part of a combination share option while keeping the remaining part).

Tactics within business are, it seems, a rich area for new terminology. In particular, those who resist a hostile takeover bid can draw on a growing lexicon of strategies with which to arm themselves. In the US, a **macaroni defense** is an anti-takeover tactic in which the cost of any takeover is substantially increased through the issue of a large number of bonds which would need to be redeemed at sale, just as macaroni expands when placed in boiling water. Meanwhile, a **Jonestown defense** involves the target company of a hostile takeover deliberately using tactics so extreme (swallowing a 'poison pill') as to threaten its viability. The term alludes to the Jonestown massacre of 1978, in which members of the People's Temple cult committed mass suicide by drinking Kool-Aid laced with cyanide.

Perhaps this striking use of language is partly the point of business speak: to give colour and vibrancy to processes which can be complex and, at times, mundane. Work and play—or at least language play—do not always need to occupy separate spaces.

**to have bench:** to have enough supporters to back up an enterprise or initiative. The idiom is one of many borrowed from sport and refers to a team's bench of supporters and substitutes.

**Pac-Man defence:** a defensive tactic against hostile takeovers in which the target firm turns the tables and attempts to take over the acquiring firm. 'Pac-Man' was an arcade game from the 1980s, in which a big dot races around a maze eating up smaller dots, trying to avoid 'ghosts' chasing it. At certain points in the game, the Pac-Man can chase and eat the ghosts.

**bottom feeder:** someone who buys a share when it is at its lowest value. The term, also used outside business contexts where it denotes a person of low status who survives by any means possible, alludes to fish such as catfish and gudgeon which feed off the bottom of a river or lake.

**vice investing:** an investment strategy that targets companies which cater to human vices such as alcohol, tobacco, and arms manufacturing. It is seen as the financial opposite of **ethical investing**.

**underload syndrome:** ill health due to a lack of motivation in the workplace.

**to kitchen-sink:** to announce all of a company's bad financial results at one time. The term alludes back to the idiom 'everything but the kitchen sink', originating during World War II to describe heavy artillery from the enemy, and describes the strategy of taking the repercussions on share value and public dissatisfaction in one hit.

**fad surfing:** the practice of adopting one fashionable management strategy after another.

**offshoring:** the practice of locating business overseas at the expense of local workforces.
In the US, where Forrester predicts 3.3m of the 130m non-farm jobs will be 'offshored' by 2015, five states are already working on banning the practice to protect local employment.
*Daily Telegraph*, 2003.

**moose on the table:** an issue which everyone in a business meeting knows is a problem but which no one wants to address. An alternative term is **moose in the room** and, in the US, **elephant in the room**.
One way of dealing with the Moose-on-the-Table is to introduce the concept to everyone in the team and play with it. It's a powerful and fun way to get serious issues out in the open. Some teams have given everyone a little stuffed moose.
Jim Clemmer, *The Leader's Digest: Timeless Principles for Team and Organization Success*, 2004.

**prawn-sandwich man** (also **prawn-sandwich brigade/prawn-sandwich world**): a corporate freeloader, particularly at sports events. The prawn sandwich has been variously used as a totem in the commercial world, perhaps most famously by Gerald Ratner who effectively destroyed his jewellery business by referring to his company's products as 'crap', and 'cheaper than a prawn sandwich'. The latest meaning was initiated by footballer Roy Keane, who complained that corporate greed was destroying professional football, as symbolized by the eating of prawn sandwiches in the directors' box at the expense of the fans on the stands.
But he isn't a prawn-sandwich man, he doesn't fit the AB1 bill, he isn't advertiser-friendly, he's the kind of fellow that they've spent the past decade desperately trying to discourage. In short, he's a Saturday man.
Patrick Collins writing in *espn.soccernet.com*.

**warm-chair attrition:** a loss in productivity due to unmotivated employees who are simply 'keeping their chair warm', waiting for another job.

**silver ceiling:** the systems or attitudes of a company which prevent older workers from advancing. The term is an extension of other 'ceilings', such as *glass ceiling* (preventing women from moving up) and *stained-glass ceiling* (obstructions to promotion within the church).

**bezzle:** an act of fraud or embezzlement. The (now obsolete) verb 'bezzle' dates back to the mid-1700s, but it has recently started to be used as a noun.

**double-hatting:** to be responsible for multiple jobs (also known as **multi-hatting**).
It strikes me this all boils down to one thing—that the Prime Minister is running out of people he can trust to do the jobs. You have all been double-hatted; you have all got flatmates at the other end doing things.
Ian Liddell-Grainger MP speaking to Alastair Darling MP at a meeting of the Select Committee of Scottish Affairs, 2003.

**neuromarketing:** the neurological study of a consumer's reactions when being exposed to marketing messages. The analysis of subconscious thoughts is carried out by **neuromarketers** with the aim of strengthening emotional bonds with their products.
There's not much profit yet in neuroeconomics' eyebrow-raising sidekick—neuromarketing—but that might not be far behind . . . Certainly we'd torture ourselves much less over a potential impulse buy if we could just know in advance whether we were going to like it or not.
Eric Roston writing in *Time* magazine, 2004.

**pension holiday:** the temporary skipping of pension contributions made by an employer in order to boost or protect its financial situation. The practice has come under fierce criticism by workers in many countries who fear a drastic reduction in funds and a lack of cover in the event of bankruptcy.

**daddy month:** a benefit offered in Sweden whereby fathers can take a month's paternity leave and receive eighty per cent of their pay. A similar plan is being considered by the British government.

**granny leave:** the option, given to carers, of working fewer hours in order to look after ageing relatives.

**portfolio worker:** a person who has multiple contracts with multiple companies.

## How to find a husband, business-style

In 2004, the publication of a single book was said to have revolutionized the twenty-first-century dating game. *The Program: How to Find a Husband after Thirty* stormed both British and American bookshops, and the media coverage it received was enormous.

The book has as its subtitle 'A 15-Step Action Plan Using What I Learned at Harvard Business School', and 'guarantees results' within twelve to eighteen months. Both statements reflect the approach of the author, Rachel Greenwald, who tackles the subject of husband-hunting by applying strategies usually confined to the business world. Her message is essentially that a woman should brand herself. As a result, the language of *The Program* is heavily influenced by the idiom of marketing, and includes sections on 'Packaging' and 'Telemarketing', as well as tips on how a woman can raise her stock in the 'Dow Jane Index'.

In Greenwald's dating context, 'mass marketing' is a process by which a woman tells everyone she knows that she is in the market for a man. She is encouraged to have a 'quarterly performance review', achieved by auditing results. A key tool for doing this, Greenwald says, is the 'exit interview' with departing boyfriends, which helps a woman measure her 'retention rate' of men.

This new approach to 'man-agement', if a rather flippant example, is nonetheless a good illustration of how business jargon is creeping into the vocabulary of other contexts, however remote from the world of commerce.

# 5

# Daggers and Diplomacy:
## The Language of Politics

**From Trotsky to tosserdom in one generation.**
Historian Peter Hennessy on the one-time 1960s' radicals who have flocked to become Labour peers.

**Michael Howard. The oldest new game show in town: 'Opportunism Knocks'.**
Deputy Prime Minister John Prescott to Labour's spring conference, March 2004, speaking of the new Leader of the Opposition and playing on the name of the 1960s' talent show *Opportunity Knocks*.

**Not so much naked opportunists but G-string opportunists: not quite bare but bare-faced.**
Former Conservative spin doctor Amanda Platell on the Tories' opposition to tuition fees.

**Sir: We have endured the word 'Blairite' all these years. Now, a new sound bite beckons. How about 'Blairrong'?**
Letter to the Editor in *The Independent*, 21 July 2003.

**Recession is when your neighbour loses his job. Depression is when you lose yours. And recovery is when Jimmy Carter loses his.**
Ronald Reagan, 1911–2004, in the 1980 US presidential campaign.

There are few areas in which language is so scrupulously analysed as in political discourse, and it would be hard to find a year in which language played a more crucial role in political life as it did in 2003. The various positions of the world's governments towards the conflict in Iraq were examined in painstaking detail, and more often than not it was the rhetoric used to communicate those positions which came under the greatest scrutiny. From the heavily religious overtones of phrases used by the US administration (**moral crusade**, **axis of evil**, **just war**), to the almost poetic anti-war rhetoric of the German and French governments, the language of war embraced far wider conflicts than those on the battlefields themselves.

As 2003 closed, in the face of mounting criticism of the war and the failure to find any **weapons of mass destruction**, the rhetoric of both George W. Bush and Tony Blair found on occasion a more tempered vocabulary. The leaders of both countries acknowledged the principles behind much of Europe's opposition, speaking of **good-faith** disagreements and moving away from the anti-French rhetoric summed up in one of the most frequently cited phrases of 2003, **cheese-eating surrender monkeys**. Yet the language of mollification was not always guaranteed; as public pressure increased, Tony Blair in particular reverted to the language of aggression and the by now familiar refrain of **the struggle between good and evil**. Military metaphors were also striking in the PM's announcement, in May 2004, of a likely British referendum on membership of the European Union: **Let the battle be joined** became the phrase of the moment on the eve of the **big bang** enlargement of the EU from fifteen to twenty-five member states.

The profiles of public figures can depend heavily upon their idiom, making the role of speechwriters a highly powerful one. 'Top politicians generally have an arm's-length acquaintance with their own language', wrote the novelist Julian Barnes, 'they only truly mean what other people help them say.' Tony Blair's speechwriters have created for him a highly personalized language, punctuated by key phrases which have marked his premiership. **New**, **tough**, **renewal**, **power**, and **equal** have all featured consistently in his speeches, forming collectively what some unconvinced pundits have termed **Blair-blur.** In the US, it was David Frum, George W. Bush's former speechwriter, who coined the phrase **axis of evil** and its original incarnation, **axis of hate**. Looking further back, John Kenneth Galbraith, the speechwriter for Adlai Stevenson who subsequently wrote for John Kennedy, related how Kennedy rejected one of the first speeches Galbraith had written for him: whilst a great speech, he said, 'It's not me, it's Adlai'.

In the run-up to the US presidential election, this role of the speechwriter became critical as the language of each of the candidates was put under
particular scrutiny. If George W. Bush was said to define the world in black

or white, the language of Democratic nominee John Kerry was full of nuance and often seemed to belie his self-promoted toughness. Some commentators preferred the bald and occasionally clumsy humour of the incumbent president ('Those weapons of mass destruction have to be somewhere', Bush quipped while showing unamused guests at a public dinner a photo of himself looking under his desk) to the less entertaining speeches of his opponent. 'All too often', wrote Rupert Cornwell in *The Independent*, 'a Kerry speech is a symphony in greys.' If Bush's mantra was **'either with us or against us'**, Kerry took a **'on the one hand . . . on the other'** approach. In the UK, the new philosophy of the Tory Party under Michael Howard emerged as **compassionate conservatism**, something which had been seen to work for Bush's Republican cause across the Atlantic.

The playwright David Edgar, writing in *The Guardian*, has made the observation that 'politico'—the jargon of the politicians—has been infiltrated by the language of commerce. Certainly British Chancellor Gordon Brown's 2004 budget speeches drew heavily on business buzzwords, with frequent references to **mergers**, **synergies**, **cost efficiencies**, and his **front office**. In the US, while perhaps unsurprising in the run-up to a presidential election when the size of campaign funds is as much a talking point as political ideology, commercial vocabulary was also made useful. Political consultants distinguished between **retail politics**, in which a campaign is built around the personal door-to-door canvassing of votes, and **wholesale politics**, which relies on more impersonal advertising via national media. The move from 'retail' to 'wholesale' has been described by some as a shift from **grassroots to Astroturf**, and by others as **mixing Politics with Primetime**.

The following terms have all found a place in the political lexicon of the twenty-first century. Some may need the application of a little **behindology**, the study of the hard political realities behind the spin (and not all are as entertaining as the latest genre in music known as **New Labour Rock**, describing pop music that tries to be both mainstream and edgy at the same time). They are divided into two camps: the first listing some of the defining terms in the run-up to the US presidential election, and the second a selection from the most recent of buzzwords from the British political arena.

# On the campaign trail

**ABC:** short for 'Anything but Clinton', and used to describe the Bush administration's agenda to run counter to the policies and principles of the previous White House incumbent.

ABC . . . remains as close as Dubya has to a North Korea policy.

*Asia Times*, August 2003.

**dirty tricks Thursday:** the Thursday before an election when candidates release scandalous stories in order to garner bad publicity for their opponent. The timing means that the accused will have little time to refute the allegations.

Arnold Schwarzenegger checks in to talk about the crescendo of personal attacks registered against him by his political foes during the past few days . . . . Polls show that 'dirty tricks Thursday' didn't work.

Headlines from the website of Talk Radio KFSO, San Francisco, November 2003.

**blue-hot:** the intensity of the reaction within the US Democratic Party to moves by the Republicans. The election map results of presidential elections show Republican states in red, and Democratic states in blue.

'The Democrats are angry', he says. 'The recall is a blue-hot issue; the Texas redistricting is a blue-hot issue. And of course, Dean is the blue-hot candidate.'

*The Christian Science Monitor*, September 2003.

**narrative politics:** a brand of politics in which more attention is paid to a politician's life story than to more traditional credentials. The term took centre stage in September 2003, when the Hollywood actor Arnold Schwarzenegger became governor of California. The style of politics was seen to be particularly appropriate to **The Governator** (a play on Schwarzenegger's most famous role as 'The Terminator'), particularly in the wake of numerous allegations of sexual harassment said to have occurred during his film career.

**Hispandering:** the paying of political attention to the needs of the Hispanic community, seen as the group which may decide the winner of the presidential election. The term is a blend of *Hispanic* and *pandering*.

**Seabiscuit** (**candidate**)**:** an election candidate who comes from behind to win. The term is a reference to the racing horse *Seabiscuit*, who became

34　a winner against all expectations and whose story was told in a book and

film of the same name. The term has been applied to John Kerry, who described himself as the 'Comeback Kerry', a play on the Clinton nickname the 'Comeback Kid'—both men came from behind to gain significant wins. I have always seen John Kerry as the Seabiscuit of this race. He's back at the third corner and he sees the wire and there goes Seabiscuit—by the time they see him, nobody can catch him.
  Max Cleland, former senator and campaigner for Kerry, as reported in the *Financial Times*, January 2004.

**packing and cracking:** the redrawing of electoral boundaries to favour one political party over another. 'Packing' refers to pulling more supporters into a district, whereas 'cracking' means splitting a constituency and preventing supporters of the opposing party from voting en masse. The term is the contemporary equivalent of the older word 'gerrymandering'.

**lawnsprinkler vote:** the vote of ordinary (often suburb-dwelling and lawn-owning) Americans, as opposed to liberals embracing more controversial causes.
Cultivated party pollsters would patiently explain how their clients planned to detach the lawnsprinkler vote from coastal feminazis.
  David Edgar writing in *The Guardian*, March 2004.

**velcroid:** a person who stands close to an important leader (especially during photo sessions) in order to achieve increased media exposure. More recently, the term has been applied to a persistent questioner. Both senses derive from the word's root, *Velcro*, the proprietary name for the adhesive material used as a fastener for clothes and other items.

**squeaker:** a close race, or 'photofinish', between political contenders.
Long known for its power in setting the national political agenda, the state of New Hampshire has weighed into the 2002 Senate battle as well, lining up a race that's expected to remain a squeaker until Election Day.
  *PBS News*, November 2002.

**purple state:** a US state in which Democrats and Republicans have equal levels of support, purple being a blend of blue and red, the respective colours of Democrat and Republican wins on the election-night map.

# The Labour lexicon

**The Big Conversation:** an exercise launched in November 2003 by Tony Blair's government to listen to the concerns of the British population on issues ranging from speed limits to stem-cell research.

For this was the first session of the first day of what Labour insists is one of the boldest, most innovative democratic exercises in British political history. As if taking its place alongside Great Britons, the Big Read and those other 21st century experiments in public participation, they are calling it the Big Conversation.

Jonathan Freedland in *The Guardian*, November 29 2003.

**The Northern Way:** a term coined by John Prescott following the model of Labour's signature 'Third Way'. It denotes collaboration between agencies and authorities in the north of Britain to bring economic regeneration to these areas. The term is also intended as a pun on the British government's idea to create a 'growth corridor' in northern Britain.

**urban village:** a way of living, promoted by key figures including Prince Charles, which aims to promote small and tightly knit communities which enjoy local self-reliance and function as units within large urban areas. The UK government has also referred to **urban** or **community coding** as the blueprints for such plans.

**New localism:** a label given to the UK government's plans to devolve new freedoms in decision-making to the best local councils.

[New] Localism is a development concept that would enable humanly-scaled, environmentally healthy, politically active, economically robust communities.

The New Rules project (a resource for policy-makers aimed at strengthening local communities).

**sustainable community:** another recent New Labour buzzword to describe a community in which all inhabitants cooperate to make it a place they are proud to live in. The US administration's equivalent terms are **liveability** and **New Urbanism**.

**civic pioneer:** a term given by Home Secretary David Blunkett to councils which are committed to developing and sustaining opportunities for local people.

**the choice doctrine:** a strategy of the Labour Party as laid out in a document entitled 'Making Choices', aimed at improving the receipt and delivery of public services. Other terms under the 'choice' umbrella include **enhanced choice** and **optional choice**.

## Politics in the kitchen

When the British Conservative Party, under William Hague, announced a strategy of **kitchen-table politics**, made up of **bread and butter** issues, political language and the language of food forged a surprising relationship. The combination was not new, however. In 1992, Labour leader John Smith's mission to charm workers in the City of London over lunch became known as the **prawn cocktail offensive**, prompting the then Deputy Prime Minister Michael Heseltine to quip 'Never have so many crustaceans died in vain'. (The culmination of the metaphorical feast was the clarion cry **'Save the prawns!'**.) The term was resurrected in 2004 when used to describe Chancellor Gordon Brown's 'sweet-talking' of the academic community. Meanwhile, Britain's current Deputy PM John Prescott recalled in the Commons a remark from the Tory peer Lord Willoughby that 'expecting to renegotiate the EU treaty on our terms is like going to McDonalds and ordering **lobster thermidor.**' 'I don't know what it is about seafood and politics', quipped Prescott, 'but I couldn't have put it better myself'.

There are many more examples. In 2001, the then Foreign Secretary Robin Cook distilled Britain's cultural identity in the dish **chicken tikka masala**, 'a perfect illustration of the way Britain absorbs and adapts external influences'. The Australian term **chardonnay socialist**, a play on **champagne socialist,** came into play to describe those on the political left with comfortable middle-class incomes, and a taste for the finer things in life. In the US, the **sushi-eating liberals** is a similarly pejorative label now thrown at the left.

▶

Sophistication of the palate does not always win votes: in one apocryphal story former Labour Party spin doctor Peter Mandelson was said to have exposed the difference between the New Labour of London's Islington and the ordinary electorate when he mistook traditional British mushy peas for guacamole at his local fish and chip shop.

There even appears to be a whole culinary lexicon of insults available to politicians, as playwright David Edgar notes. Campaign strategists in particular have hijacked terms such as **frying, broiling, creaming, toasting** or **shish-kebabbing** when rallying against their electoral opponents—often by way of 'handing their asses to them **on a platter**'.

# 6

# Words on a Plate:
## Food and Drink

To read the food pages of the broadsheet papers you would think that . . . tonno e fagioli was as popular as fish and chips.

> Julian Baggini in *The Guardian*, March 2004.

I think it's impossible to make gin fashionable. Bombay Sapphire? That one word says it all—it's Daily Telegraph obituary page commentators!

> Wine critic Malcolm Gluck, March 2004.

I don't want to have to refer to my French fry potatoes as freedom fries, and I don't want to have to freedom kiss my wife.

> Woody Allen, June 2003.

#### Lifting the new lids on the bloc

> Headline in *The Times* in April 2004 on the likely influence of new cuisines from the ten countries which were to join the European Union on 1 May.

The linguistic and gastronomic identities of English-speaking nations often have much in common. The integration of words we borrow from abroad is as certain and continuous as our absorption of cuisines. Words, and dishes, can be imported wholesale, or adapted to the tastes of their new co-owners. In 2001 and in a speech to celebrate Britishness, the then Foreign Secretary Robin Cook illustrated the British ability to assimilate and adapt external influences with the example of **chicken tikka masala** (see page 37). 'Chicken Tikka is an Indian dish,' he said, 'The Masala sauce was added to satisfy the desire of British people to have their meat served in gravy.'

The influences of other countries on our language and on our palates often meet: many of the food and drink terms we use and encounter had their origins elsewhere. These terms are very often the same as in their native country, and are kept in part because of the exotic, 'echt', appeal of their names. Recent Japanese imports offer a good example: **nigiri sushi** (pieces of **sashimi** on a bed of rice, often held together by **nori**, toasted sheets of seaweed), **dashi** (fish and seaweed stock), **ponzu** (a dipping sauce made from soy sauce, lime juice, and fish flakes), and **enoki** (tiny mushrooms), have retained their original names and boosted their exotic appeal. **Body sushi**, on the other hand, is perhaps exotic enough in itself to warrant its straightforward English name: the practice involves the eating of sushi off the body of a naked woman and is said to draw on an ancient Japanese custom known as **nyotai mori**.

In parallel with this introduction of unadulterated imports, chefs in the adopting countries have been creating new variations on the cuisine they have taken in. If, throughout the world, sushi remains vinegared rice served with raw fish or other ingredients, the difference in regional and national styles can be enormous—a **California roll** (a sushi roll which is made inside out) and a **Philadelphia roll** (containing cream cheese) are wholly American takes on Japanese cuisine. Mexican food provides another illustration. The standard fare of Mexican cuisine—**burritos**, **enchiladas**, **tacos**, and **tamales**—all have nineteenth- or early twentieth-century attestation for their first adoption into English. As these have become naturalized so other dishes have been created in their new environment: **chilaquiles**, **chimichanga**, **chipotle**, **fajita**, **flauta**, and **tostaguac** are all becoming commonplace items on American menus.

The difference between these last examples and those of the California and Philadelphia rolls is that the 'new Mexicans' have all the resonance of their geographical origins in their names, whether or not the results are 'pure' Spanish. This trend towards keeping native names for borrowed foods is evident in another way. Some dishes, having been re-christened soon after their arrival, have been re-acquiring their original names, undergoing a form of 'exotic reintroduction'. **Perilla**, an Asian aromatic herb and popular particularly in the US, is attested in English as far back as the late eighteenth century. Recently, however, it has begun to be marketed as
40  **shisho**, its Japanese name. This renaming, among other things, enables it

to command a high price in Asian markets in spite of its ready availability in the wild, even on roadsides. Other American renamings in the twentieth century also fit this pattern. Until 1960, the herb **arugula** was known as **rocket** in the US, as it is still in the UK. 'Arugula', the Italian name for the herb, has now vanquished all competition. Staying with herbs, Americans used **coriander** throughout the nineteenth century, but today—probably owing to the influence and popularity of Mexican cuisine in the US—most Americans use the herb's Spanish name **cilantro** (albeit retaining 'coriander' for the seed).

Trends in food and drink can change as often as fashion, and the need for novelty and fresh interest is just as important. Glamorizing more prosaic foodstuffs by giving them 'faux elegant' names is not new, and is a pattern continuing today. The latest drink to arrive from Asia is **bubble tea**, cold tea which is sweetened, flavoured, and shaken until frothy. Known also as **boba** tea, it is notable for the tiny tapioca balls which are sucked up through a wide straw. These balls used to be a snack for Taiwanese children, until a clever marketer renamed them 'boba', a Taiwanese word connoting the image of a busty woman. Less entertainingly, the **Chilean sea bass** is in fact not a sea bass at all, but the **Patagonian toothfish**, while the poetic note struck by the **golden snapper** would have been absent from its more prosaic name **tilefish**. In the same way, the Japanese **gyoza** is an alternative for the coarser-sounding **pot-sticker**, **soba** (also Japanese) nicely replaces **buckwheat noodles**, **bresaola** is essentially the same as the far plainer **beef jerky**, and **ajinomoto** deftly glosses over the associations of the much-criticized **monosodium glutamate** or **MSG**. Finally, it has lately been noticed that a native American product, country ham, is indistinguishable from prosciutto if sliced thinly enough. As a result, it is being marketed as **American prosciutto**.

2004 provided a nice counterpoint to such attempts to sanitize food and drink terms. A rather more earthy approach was heralded in a headline in *The Guardian* which ran: 'As farm produce gets fruitier, plum becomes just another four-letter word'. Its story covered the reintroduction in Britain of some of the country's rarest apples, pears, and plums, some of which carry names that are a little less than refined. Ancient varieties such as **Hen's Turd** and **Kill-Boy** apples, **Shit Smock** plums, and **Bloody Bastard** pears, are putting pressure on the more pleasant and rural sounding **Orange Pippin** and **Egremont Russet** apples, and **Maiden's Blush** plums.

◎

On the accession of ten new states to the European Union on 1 May 2004, the British weekly shopping baskets looked about to be revolutionized by the availability of new cuisines. Within days the first Baltic range of meals to be sold in a major supermarket was announced, while British diplomats tipped the **potica**, a traditional yeast roll filled with walnuts and raisins, to become a new favourite across Europe. The same was forecast for Polish **pierogi** ('little pies'), and the Lithuanian **dzukian**, 'potato pie'.

◎

One subject which preoccupied headline writers was that of obesity, and the warnings from nutritionists of a potential pandemic which they coined **globesity**. In 2004, the fast-food chain McDonalds launched a range of salads in addition to its more traditional fare, a strategy which got off to a shaky start when some of its new 'healthy' options were found to contain more fat than a hamburger (a gaffe which prompted the *Mirror* newspaper to quip 'Fail Caesar'). Governments began to talk about **fat** and **junk food taxes**, and the Atkins Diet became a multi-billion-pound industry, with food shops and restaurants rapidly joining in on the **low-carb** approach. Many fast-food chains quickly came up with dishes catering to those trying to avoid conventional carbohydrates; one major hamburger chain, for example, began to offer an Angus beef beefburger wrapped only in lettuce.

◎

Meanwhile, for the first time in fifty years, gin was left out of the virtual shopping basket filled annually by the Office of National Statistics to demonstrate the eating habits of the British nation. The spirit was overtaken by vodka. If now out of favour, gin has nevertheless a fascinating linguistic history. In the eighteenth century there were said to be more than 17,000 gin houses in London, then a city of 700,000 people. Gaudily decorated public houses were known as 'gin palaces'. The drink acquired numerous nicknames—both as a sign of affection and as euphemisms for something said at the time to cause death, debauchery, and even spontaneous combustion. **Cuckold's Comfort**, **Mother's Ruin**, **My Lady's Eye-Water**, **Cock-my-Cap**, and **Royal Poverty** were just some of gin's highly colourful epithets. If gin looked to be going out of favour, another spirit came surprisingly back in. Cognac, sales of which had been steadily declining, has become the favourite tipple of 'gangsta' rappers. A favourite brand is Hennessy, referred to in lyrics as **Henny**, **Henn-dog** and **Henn-roc**.

## Tip of the iceberg: the new face of lettuce

In the 1960s the iceberg lettuce took top position in the salad bowls of the British and Americans nations, thanks to its durability. It went on to be disdained as the cheaper and tasteless alternative to other, more exotic leaves. Now enjoying something of a comeback, it coexists today with a myriad of salad leaves which have firmly established themselves on even the smallest of supermarket shelves. The following lists only a selection of those available to us today, thanks to the high exposure of television chefs and to our abiding interest in exotic foods.

**rocket:** strong and peppery

**cos:** firm, with a subtle nutty flavour

**frisée:** feathery, curly, and bitter

**escarole:** crisp and mild

**lollo rosso:** red, heavily ruffled, and mild

**mizuna:** hot and mustardy

**mesclun:** mixed leaves, both peppery and mild

**radicchio:** bright red member of chicory family

**red mustard:** mild mustard flavour

**lamb's lettuce** (also **mâche**): soft, spoon-shaped and nutty

**ruby chard:** bright red, glossy, and sharp-tasting

**sweet romaine:** sweet and crisp

# 7

# Words in the Wardrobe:
## The Language of Fashion

**A shell-suit wearing dolewaller with a bum fluff 'tache and fake bling-bling jewellery attempts to tap-up a pram-pushing teenage slapper with a Croydon facelift.**

*Front* magazine, as reported in *www.Lazycinema.com*, September 2003.

**An extraordinary explosion of G-strings, tassels, boas and bustiers.**

*Daily Mirror*, March 2004, on the Californian 'Miss America of Burlesque' competition.

**Beckalaureate**
The title of a new three-year degree offered by Kuala Lumpur Metropolitan University and devoted to the study of David Beckham. Modules include 'Big hair: the efficacy of constant change'.

Reported in *The Loof Daily*, Malaysia, on April Fool's Day, 2004.

**They've trodden the fine line between being very smart, and 'Footballers' Wives'.**

Editor of British *Vogue*, Alexandra Shulman, on the Burberry label.

**A typical *Sex and the City* scenario showed one of Carrie's boyfriends laughing at her hat. Though she took it off, you knew it would be the man who would go in the end.**

Natasha Walter writing in *The Guardian*, March 2004.

The vocabulary of fashion is as eclectic and varied as the world it describes. The creation of new styles, the resurrection of trends from the past, and the infinite potential combinations of both, are a mirror image on a small scale of the way in which language evolves. Most of the new words in use today are simply older words back in the news, or a combination of existing elements which together create something different.

In 2003 and 2004, the fashions of the moment included (among many others) the burlesque, the 'goddess' (draping, one-shoulder, ruched dresses), and styles with twists from both the 1950s and the 1920s. Drop-waist dresses added a modern flapper edge to the catwalks, while *full circle skirts* were seen for a time as the perfect partywear. As ever, it was the fashion icons who directed tastes more than the catwalk. David Beckham, at least until his alleged fall from grace, was seen by many to have redefined the role of a style-conscious modern man (or *metrosexual*) by dint of his ever-changing hairstyles and daring fashion flirtations. Films such as *Starsky and Hutch*, a remake of the popular and iconic 1970s TV series, and of-the-moment TV programmes such as *Sex and the City* (*SATC*), proved as influential on a nation's wardrobe as anything seen in the top fashion shows. Newspaper fashion editors shared the secret of where to find the 'supercool shades', flares, or exact brand of sneakers sported in the former, while corsages, prom skirts, baguette bags, and dangly earrings were all said to have been reinvigorated by *SATC*. Such slavish following of fashions seen on the small screen did not amuse everybody, and some lamented what was termed a 'monkey-see-monkey' approach to fashion and entertainment.

Linguistically, fashion has seen a return of many terms from the past, some with an interesting history. *Piecrust collars*, for example, named for the starchy frill around a high neckline which resembles fluted pastry, saw a (for many unwelcome) return. The *Oxford English Dictionary* first dates the attributive *pie-crust,* used to describe something having an ornamental edge, to 1902. Another trend to be revived in the 2000s was the *rockabilly*, a term dating back to 1956 and describing the musical hybrid of rock and roll and hillbilly (the term *billy* meaning 'brother' or 'friend').

Like the music, the fashion of rockabilly—based on American college classics combined with elements of rock and biking culture—was meant to denote nonconformity. The status reflected by a person's choice of clothing was the subject of much discussion in 2004, when the dress code of the so-called *chav* (see pages 142–143) came under scrutiny. With the very public analysis of *chavdom* arrived a perceived partnership between class and fashion which for decades had flown beneath the radar (with the exception perhaps of *Essex Girl* and *trailer trash*). References were made to *council house chic*, a style taken to be as serious an indicator of social status as the wearing of Burberry raincoats by *townies*. Both 'chavs' and 'townies' are wearers of brands which were once the domain of the well-to-do, but which have gone onto acquire associations of hooliganism and thuggishness—the famous Burberry check was recently described by the *The Guardian* as 'the ultimate symbol of nouveau riche naff'. Both groups also see themselves as the natural enemies of *grungers*, *skaters*, and *goths*, groups whose status is equally distilled in their respective fashion choices. Those who choose not to follow any trend and to wear exactly what they like, however they wish to wear it, have become known as *free-stylers*.

The following offers a selection of words circulating the fashion world. Like the articles and trends they describe, some may already be out of date, but may well resurface in years to come.

**mini-crini:** a design pioneered by British fashion designer Vivienne Westwood in 1985, featuring small-shouldered and full-skirted dresses. At the time these were at odds with the prevailing fashion of broad shoulders and pencil skirts. The style has become a talking point again with the retrospective of Westwood's work at London's Victoria and Albert Museum.

**prairie chic:** the style of settlers in the American prairie, in which 'baker-boy caps' (flat caps once worn by delivery boys), floral dresses, aprons, and flat, round-toed boots feature large.
The 'prairie chic' look emerged back in the summer, when trendy Notting Hillbillies began to wear hand-me-down style frocks or aprons over dark denim jeans.
   *Daily Telegraph*, November 2003.

**council house facelift**, also known as the **Croydon facelift** (referring to the London suburb of Croydon, associated in this sense with being lower class): hair pulled back in an ultra-tight bun, pulling the skin of the face and forehead up and back. Both terms are viewed as derogatory.

**eye jewels:** specially developed jewellery, including designs such as a glittering half-moon or heart, which are implanted under the cornea. Pioneered in Holland in 2004, the fashion has been much criticized by eye specialists.

**Havaiana sandals:** sandals produced in Brazil which became high fashion in Britain in the summer of 2004. They are essentially flip-flops made of natural Brazilian rubber and have been a cult in Brazil for decades.

So the flip-flop that took over the world is a rag trade to riches story with an eternal theme—that even as we pound the city streets, we dream of the beach. Slip into a pair of Havaianas, and in some indefinable way, you become an honorary Brazilian.

Oliver Bennett in *The Times*, 2004.

**masstige** (a blend of mass market and prestige)**:** a retail category consisting of prestige product concepts created and developed for mass brands.

**hairt:** a hat that looks like an extension of one's own hair.

Next time you suffer a bad hair day, why not try a 'hairt'? The hat that thinks it's a hairstyle is a new concept of millinery.

*Daily Telegraph*, November 2003.

**handcuff bracelets:** locking bracelets worn by two people as a symbol of love and commitment. A recent advertisement by the jewellers Cartier caused a stir because of its choice of two women to model its new $4,000 handcuff bracelets.

**joggies:** people (especially teenagers) who wear hooded jogging tops. This latest transferred sense has not yet superseded the more established one of tracksuit bottoms, but it carries the same imputation of a working-class wearer.

**prison-whites:** trainers which are kept in pristine, white, condition, and favoured particularly by rap stars and their followers.

They are the sullen, pasty-faced youths in hooded tops and spanking-new 'prison whites' who loiter listlessly on street corners.

Opinion piece in the *Daily Telegraph*, February 2004, titled 'In Defence of Snobbery'.

**coffee tights:** tights which are impregnated with coffee, and which are said to reduce cellulite in a woman's legs by absorption of caffeine into the skin.

Instant coffee is passé-pasta, now 'thinstant coffee' is here to stay. An Austrian firm Palmers has succeeded in making 'Coffee Tights', which trim women's

legs by stimulating the breakdown of fat, according to a report in the Sun.
*Times of India*, March 2004.

**semi-fro:** a hairstyle that is almost 'Afro'. This is one of a number of
'-fro' compounds emerging, including **lo-fro** and **Jewfro**.
The allure he held for females despite his short stature and nappy semi-fro was
always a mystery.
Chat-room conversation, 2004.

**biniki:** a support device for the buttocks designed to give them a firm
shape. The generic term **butt-bra** is also becoming popular.

**Mary Janes:** shoes with straps across the instep which are traditionally
round-toed and low. Modern versions vary widely but the basic style was
much popularized by the TV series *Sex and the City*.

**pelmet** (short for 'pelmet skirt'): a very short miniskirt.

**rah-rah skirt:** a full, frilly, and short skirt which was high fashion in
the 1980s, having peviously been worn typically by cheerleaders. It has
recently staged a comeback.

**eVest** (US; also the **Scott eVest**): a vest or waistcoat which has multiple
pockets in which to store electronic devices such as mobile phones, MP3
players, and PDAs (personal digital assistants).
The eVest is enough to give even Bill Gates a wet dream. It has pockets for all
your gear, and is designed to be wireless with every cable running through the
lining of the jacket.
*Boys Toys*, 2003.

**wifebeater** (Australia/New Zealand): a man's vest or short-sleeved
T shirt. The connotations of the term have, not surprisingly, caused
controversy, particularly in the US.

# 8

# Language with Muscle:
## Sport and Fitness

**Sport is an inarticulate human expression and its practitioners should not be condemned for being, a lot of the time, pretty inarticulate.**
Rod Liddle in *The Times*, April 2004.

**Racing drivers have balls, but none of them are crystal, so seeing into the future is a little bit difficult.**
David Coulthard, Formula 1 driver, after being dropped by the McLaren racing team.

**Who's the fat bloke in the number eight shirt?**
Headline in *The Guardian*, February 2004, after a clothes historian discovers that Henry VIII owned a pair of football boots.

**'Result of one mile', blared the loud-speaker, 'time three minutes . . .'. The rest was lost in the roar of the crowd.**
A description in *The Times* on the 50th anniversary of Roger Bannister's four-minute mile on 6 May 2004.

The language of sport moves slowly. Within established areas the terminology remains remarkably constant in comparison with other fields of human activity, and it is largely left to new sports (especially of the extreme kind) to generate new vocabulary. The reason for this is uncertain, although some would stress that the focus of players is on physical rather than verbal expression. A less generous analysis would look to the inarticulateness of players and others involved in the game, and their reliance on age-worn clichés such as 'the boy done good'.

Whatever the reason, and in spite of the high drama of great sporting moments, sporting idiom remains highly conservative. When a new usage does become established, it is inevitably 'parroted' by fans in thousands of after-match pub conversations: two examples are the use of **quality** and **class** as adjectives, as in 'He will always score goals for us because he's quality' and 'The top teams have four class strikers'.

## Some of the top football clichés

Teams often **hit a rich vein of form**. Managers always **take each game as it comes**. Relegation games against near-rivals will always be **six-pointers**. Unfortunately for Grimsby Town, their team is always seen as the archetypal lower-league team: so a manager might say **No disrespect to the likes of Grimsby**, while if a team is relegated it has to **start checking the route to Grimsby**. Inferior teams might also use **Route One** or **hoofing** tactics, whereas a **footballing** team (who in fact **like to play football**), are known for their **silky** passing.

The football season is always **a marathon not a sprint**, and will more often than not **go to the wire**. Hard-working players **cover every blade of grass**, they have a **good engine**, and can **do a job for you**. If they are injured in the process, the rest of the team is **sweating on their fitness**.

Two soccer managers who have bucked the trend of saying as little as possible, as unoriginally as possible, are Claudio Ranieri of Chelsea and Gordon Strachan, who resigned as manager of Southampton after a very successful season in which the club reached the FA Cup final and finished eighth in the Premier League. Strachan, a Scot who wears his heart on his sleeve, became particularly well known for his honest, often humorous responses to questions and his refusal to take refuge in cliché, as in the following exchanges:

*Reporter:* Gordon, you must be delighted with that result?
*Strachan:* You're spot on! You can read me like a book.

*Reporter:* This might sound like a daft question, but you'll be happy to get your
50   first win under your belt, won't you?

*Strachan:* You're right. It is a daft question. I'm not even going to bother answering that one. It is a daft question, you're spot on there.

Such welcome humour is also to be found in the network of unofficial supporters' fanzines, both paper and virtual, which celebrate their club's local identity and often rather unsuccessful history in surreal and self-deprecating fashion. As top-level football becomes ever richer and more removed from the ordinary fan, with many of the stars foreign and match tickets unaffordable, there has been a resurgence of enthusiasm for the grass roots of football. The book *Fever Pitch* (1992) by Nick Hornby, while documenting the author's love for Arsenal (Premier League champions in 2004), influenced many people to write about the game in a more personal way.

Notable examples of such Internet fanzines are Yeovil Town's *Ciderspace* and Grimsby Town's *Electronic Fishcake*. Publications such as these revel in the trivia and absurdity of football, and often use nostalgic terms such as **knee-knack** and **Chinese burn**, redolent of a million 1970s childhoods. This extract from Chester City's *The Onion Bag* (an old-fashioned term for the goal net) gives the ironic flavour:

Mattie has a most distinctive running style. With chest pushed out and arms relatively motionless by his side, it is positively Neanderthal. In a previous incarnation, he was a goldfish.

Interestingly, the mainstream media have taken on something of this irreverent style in their reporting of the game, notably *The Guardian* newspaper, with comments such as:

The latest men to be linked with a move to Old Trafford are Roberto 'Thunderthighs' Carlos (again) and Alan 'Is She Really Going Out With Him?' Smith (again).

In the US, 2004 saw the continued proliferation of sports-star nicknames based on the model of **A-Rod** (the star baseball player Alex Rodriguez). Other players sporting names based on the initial-letter or initial-syllable approach include **T-Mac** (Tracy McGrady, basketball), **J-Will** (Jason Williams, basketball), **D-Fish** (Derek Fisher, basketball), and **C-Webb** (Chris Webber, basketball).

If entirely new terms in sport are rare, cricket has in the last few years proved one of the exceptions to the rule, reflecting some creative word-coining as new techniques are born:

## One, doosra, teesra

In 2004, the term **doosra** was the new cricketing term on everyone's lips. Describing a method of spin bowling in which the ball spins away from the right-handed bowler as a result of his straightening his arm by more than ten degrees, 'doosra' is Urdu for 'the second' or 'the other'. It came into prominence in 2004 when the technique of the popular Sri Lankan Muttiah Muralitharan was pronounced unlawful by the International Cricket Council. Meanwhile, Pakistani off-spinner Saqlain Mushtaq was said to be developing another new delivery, one which he called the **teesra** which translates as 'the third one'.

The term **jaffa**, denoting an unplayable delivery, also suggests an interesting origin, coming perhaps from the sense of the ball being 'juicy'. A **flipper**, meanwhile, does what it says on the tin: it is a ball which pitches the same length as the previous delivery but which skids lower and faster, thereby catching an unsuspecting batsman LBW (leg before wicket).

The flipper is the most talked-about weapon in the armoury of the bowler Shane Warne, said to be responsible, almost single-handedly, for revitalizing the art of leg spin bowling. He is also the master of the **zooter**, which follows a delivery that has spun to the off or to the leg. Confident that the next ball will behave in much the same way, the batsman awaits the spin of the ball, but is deceived by the 'zooter' which does not deviate in any way, and which again 'wraps the pads' for LBW.

**Performance-enhancing drugs** continued to occupy headline space in 2004. Such is the frequency with which we encounter the term today, we tend to forget that both the phrase and the phenomenon are relatively new: 'performance-enhancing' was only added to the *Oxford English Dictionary* in 2001, with its first recorded citation dating to 1979 in reference to boxing. 'Performance drug' seems to have become an umbrella term for a number of substances taken by athletes and body-builders, whether legally or otherwise, to enhance endurance and stamina. Top of this list is **androstenedione**, or **andro** for short. Meanwhile, **roasting** (a term for 'gang rape') and **dogging** (having sex outdoors), were two further terms which took on unfortunate sporting associations as a result of the headline-grabbing activities in which some footballers were said to have participated.

English is full of terms which have travelled beyond sport to become part of general vocabulary. A recent example is **smackdown**, a term from wrestling which is increasingly being used in figurative senses. In March 2004, the *Wall Street Journal* published an article entitled 'Scalia's Smackdown', referring to Supreme Court Justice Antonin Scalia, who refused to withdraw from a case in which he was accused of being biased, and describing it as a 'smackdown for the ages'. Meanwhile the idiom **cowboy up** is another example from the US of sporting terms making wider impact. Meaning to mount a brave effort to overcome a formidable obstacle, it first came to prominence just before the 2003 World Series in baseball, with reference to the underdogs the Boston Red Sox. It has subsequently migrated to other sports: 'Welcome to Dallas Mr. Daniels, and welcome to the NBA. Cowboy Up Baby,' declared a recent article on the online basketball forum *HOOPSWORLD.com*. Its trajectory is likely to take it into mainstream use, and it is already showing signs of deliberately facetious applications, in which it means literally 'to dress up as a cowboy' ('Cowboy up. And be a man,' exhorts a rodeo blog). Finally, another term gaining currency is **X next to your name**. The 'X' in question indicates a success in a tournament or play-off, and a progression to the next stage. 'I don't want to coast in,' said the coach of the Portland Pirates hockey team in 2003, 'I want to work to get that X next to our name that we made the playoffs'.

## Yoga with everything

If sport draws largely upon its existing lexicon, the vocabulary of health and fitness is moving at a dramatically different pace as new practices emerge. Yoga in particular is generating a myriad of new terms: available to us now are **rock yoga**, **yogabeat**, **kick yoga**, **ballet yoga**, and even **yogilates** (a blend of yoga and Pilates, described by some enthusiasts as **yogatastic**). **Bikram yoga** also hit the headlines in 2004, both for what it involves—practising yoga in a studio heated to 40°C—as well as for an attempt by a millionaire yoga guru to copyright twenty-seven positions within it. **Mallakhamb** also emerged, a traditional Indian sport and competitive form of yoga performed on a rope against the clock. **Anusara**, yet another yoga variation, is based on the teaching of innovative alignment techniques; together with **ashtanga** (also known as **power yoga**) and **kundalini**, it emphasizes the meditative, spiritual, aspects of yoga as opposed to the physical.

# 9

# Hackers, Crackers, Lamers, and Gamers:
## Language Online

**That word 'cool'—it keeps cropping up. It is to Poddism what 'pious' is to Catholicism.**
Stephen Moss, *The Guardian*, January 2004, in an article entitled 'Ipod—therefore I am'.

**Would you buy a Honda with a one-gallon gas tank?**
Alan Kay, one of the earliest pioneers of personal computing, on the original Mac, which celebrated Its 20th blrthday on 24 January 2004.

The opportunities for today's new words to take hold are unprecedented in number and variety. Thanks to our new media these words can come from almost any sphere or subject, but the vocabulary that has evolved for online communities themselves has particular potential. Many predict that a single global language will be the most likely, and remarkable, result of our communication over the Web—certainly over eighty per cent of the information stored on the world's computers is estimated to be in English. What this belies, however, is the number of virtual communities who use language to create or to reinforce their identity. The result is a number of fragmented, and highly personalized, lexicons, ranging from the now well-established conventions of SMS (short message system) language to the more recent 'leetspeak' (see below). If these have become more accessible to those outside their original communities, new forms are still evolving to keep the purists ahead of the game.

In parallel, new hierarchies of participants in these distinct virtual worlds are emerging. Simple labels have been around for some time—**hackers** and **phreaks** (who illegally manipulate telephone systems) were classifications from more than three decades ago, and are joined today by the **lurkers**, **lusers** and **trolls** of chat rooms, and the **griefers**, **macroers**, and **exploiters** of virtual online games. Many of the newer classes of players, however, are defined by their status, be they a **newbie**, a **lamer**, a **muggle**, or a **leet**. Even outside the realm of games, the result suggests a fictional world of many characters, each of whom is assigned a role in their virtual community.

These and other terms from a wide variety of online forums are described below.

**sha-mail:** a Japanese term for picture mail, the taking and sending of pictures or digital images by means of inbuilt cameras in mobile phones.

**wiki:** a website which can be edited by anyone, and on which the processes of editing and reading are linked, thus avoiding the need for continuous uploading. 'Wiki' started out as one site, created by Ward Cunningham in 1995 and called the *WikiWikiWeb*, taking its name from the phrase 'wiki wiki' in Hawaiian, meaning 'quick'. Current wikis cover subjects as diverse as holidays and Tolkien. Perhaps the best known is *Wikipedia*, a comprehensive online encyclopedia to which visitors can contribute their own definitions.

**poddies:** slang term for users of iPods, palm-sized digital music players which can store up to 10,000 songs and music tracks downloaded from the Internet. An **iPod nod** is a passing nod to other wearers of the iPod's trademark white headphones.

**vlogging** (a blend of 'video' and 'blogging', its pronunciation following the model of the latter)**:** the sending of video footage from a mobile phone to a personal journal or weblog. The term is a good example of language on the move—it has evolved from the coinage 'moblogging': the sending of pictures and text to weblogs via a mobile phone, which although relatively recent is already generating new formations.

**cracker:** one who breaks security on a system. The term (a blend of 'criminal' and 'hacker') was coined in 1985 by a group of hackers in protest at journalistic misuse of the very word 'hacker', and describes someone who attempts to infiltrate official websites, thereby compromising security. The act of accessing sites without permission is expressed as **cracking**, and is alternatively known as **black-hat hacking** and **dark-side hacking** (the former because of the black hats worn by villains in cowboy films, and the latter in reference to the character Darth Vader in the 'Star Wars' films, who 'turned to the dark side').

**lamer:** a term used particularly on online bulletin boards to denote someone lacking in maturity or intelligence. Denoting the opposite of those who consider themselves **leet** (for 'elite', see below), the noun may have originated in skateboarding slang, as a description of someone too 'lame' to compete.

You're a lamer if . . . you flood a channel with text. Extra lamer points if you return to flood again after getting kicked or killed.

*www.lamers.org.uk*

**gamer:** one who plays and enjoys games. Although a general term, it is most often used today to describe participants in computer games, role-playing games (such as **MMORPGs**, or Massive Multi-Player Online Role-Playing Games), and video games.

**muggle:** a 'non-wizard'; a person lacking in skill, or who is computer-illiterate. The term comes from the Harry Potter works of J. K. Rowling, a world in which 'muggles' and 'wizards' coexist without really understanding each other. Within the computing world, 'muggle' is a modern and less disparaging successor to the term 'luser' (a contraction of 'lame user', coined in 1975), and hackers in particular use this metaphor to form compounds such as **muggle-friendly**.

**whitelisting:** the use of anti-spam filtering software to allow only specified email addresses to get through. The word follows the pattern of 'blacklisting'.

**mundane:** a person who is not employed in the computer industry. It is used more figuratively to describe someone with little computer know-how (like 'muggle', above). The word in standard English is an adjective; it was first used as a noun to describe someone who is not a devotee of science fiction, a use which continues today alongside this more recent one.

**WiLDing** (Wireless LAN Driving), also known as **war driving** and **LAN-jacking:** the activity of driving around with a portable computer or GPS (Global Positioning System) device, scanning for open wireless networks. 'LAN' stands for 'local area network'. The process is similar to that of a radio scanner, and is the modern successor to **demon dialling** in the 1980s, which involved the random dialling of multiple phone lines in order to find available data lines which could be hacked into. In the case of WiLDing, hackers are searching for wireless networks in order to gain anonymous and free high-speed Internet access. **Warchalking** is another related term, whereby a recognized set of symbols are drawn in public places to tip off others to the location of an open Wi-Fi (wireless fidelity) network, thus again enabling free Internet access.

**The U.S. Secret Service has hooked up Pringles cans to notebook computers equipped with wireless LAN access cards and begun 'war driving' around Washington and other cities in an effort to sniff out unsecured WLANs.**

*Computer World*, October 2002.

**script kiddie:** someone unskilled who downloads and uses a program or 'script' devised by a hacker or cracker with the purpose of compromising a computer system.

**flame bait:** a posting meant to incite hostile and insulting messages on an Internet discussion board. Such a message is called a **flame**, posted by **flamers** in an effort to establish superiority. A series of such messages is called a **flame war** (of which one of the most famous was the 1996 'Meow war' between a group of Harvard students and the 'Meowers', in which the students invaded the latter group's bulletin board). If a 'flamer' merely wishes to insult members of the forum, they are known as **trolls**.

**Flame Bait. Put your peril-proof sunglasses on before reading. Here's where we put those topics that seem to be attracting the most acrimonious debate.**

Bulletin board, March 2004.

**newbie** (or **newbee**): a newcomer to a particular online forum or community, such as a weblog or a newsgroup. The term is often used pejoratively to describe an ingénue who asks silly questions and who is generally uncool. A 'newbie' who shows some sign of savvy is known as a **cluebie**.

**reg:** a regular poster in a newsgroup, chat room or any kind of online community.

**Oh ya I was once a newbee too as a lot of the old regs started out also . . . . but I grew to learn from the old regs in chat, I watched, I surfed and I learned quickly.**

Discussion forum on *www.HelpBytes.co.uk*

**vote bondsac:** originally posted on LiveJournal (a website which enables the setting up of weblogs), and quickly spreading to forums, web journals, and chat rooms, this term is used as a sign-off at the end of a message in the sense of another often-used term 'peace out'. Bondsac appears to be a person, but little more is known about the phrase's origin.

**dictionary attack:** an assault on a company's server, in which the 'spammer' attaches random email prefixes to a domain name, thereby generating a list of 'live' email addresses which can be sold on or used for subsequent spam attacks. The term also has the associated meaning of breaking a cipher by running through a list of likely keys: dictionary attacks of this kind in the past include those by British code breakers of the German Enigma-ciphered messages during the Second World War.

## w00t! Speaking leet, or l33t.

Also known as 'leet', 'hexspeak', or 'hakspeak', **leetspeak** is a form of written slang or code in which a user replaces letters or other characters with numbers or non-alphabet characters, often those which bear some resemblance to the letters they are replacing (such as 4 for 'A', etc.). Like all slang, it is used as a cipher to exclude those who don't belong, particularly 'newbies' ('n00bs'). Many new forms of 'leet' are increasingly impenetrable to the outsider.

The term 'leet' comes from the word 'elite', and is thought to have originated in bulletin-board systems from the 1980s and early 1990s, where having 'elite' status allowed a user access to an exclusive set of games, software, and special chat rooms. Some conjecture that it may also have developed to defeat text filters devised for message boards in order to screen the discussion of taboo subjects.

If new and more complex forms of 'leet' are being developed, some of it is nonetheless making its way into the mainstream. Leet language is often used to shorten messages, in the same way as SMS language meets the need for concision on mobile phones. It is in fact now a popular adjunct to SMS, and has recently further

▶

entrenched its position in the mainstream through its use in such webcomics as *Megatokyo*. Simple forms of leet are also being used in the workplace as employees try to deceive company email filters through the use of creative spellings. There is even a Google search engine dedicated exclusively to searches in 'leet'.

In addition to the like-for-like replacement of letters with numbers, which purists would say is the only true form of 'leet', some of the major characteristics of alternative 'leetspeak' include the transposition of letters—so 'you' may be spelled 'yuo' and 'the' as 'teh', contractions such as 'lke' for 'like' (a convention common to texting), the use of symbols which have the appearance of the letter they are coding (so >< for 'x' and |2 for 'R'), and the capitalizing of every other letter, known sometimes as 'studlycaps'. Another convention is the overuse of exclamation marks, as in w00t!!!!!— w00t being a leet word derived from 'hoot' and defined as 'yay'—a shout of joy or victory.

# 10

# Virtual Conversations

Homer: What's an email?
Lenny: It's a computer thing, like, er, an electronic letter.
Carl: Or a quiet phone call.
    From an episode of Fox TV's *The Simpsons*

Within a remarkably short time, email and texting have come to dominate the ways in which we communicate, in some cases threatening to supplant media we have relied upon for decades. With the influence of online forums such as chat rooms, bulletin boards, and weblogs, our written language looks set to change fundamentally, perhaps irrevocably.

Viewing online and electronic language as exclusively 'written' denies in some ways the feel of these new conversations, which rely heavily on characteristics from spoken language. While writing for the Web is not significantly different from other traditional writing contexts, save for some modifications for an electronic medium—the length of text is more important, for example, if the need for scrolling down a page is to be avoided—the situations of email, texting, chat rooms, and weblogs are much closer to spoken conversation, particularly if they are going on in 'real time'. Key to this is the sense of immediacy. Online and text-message conversations, while technically letter-writing, demand a response more or less straightaway. They are also, by virtue both of their platform and their content, more transient. It is because of this sense of immediacy and impermanence that the 'chatters' allow themselves far greater informality than they are likely to do on physical paper. Messages have a momentum and an energy characteristic of one-to-one chat. As David Crystal in his study *Language and the Internet* points out, 'the whole thrust of language in such situations is spoken in character'.

Each medium's position on the speech/writing spectrum determines to a very large extent the style, vocabulary, and syntax used within them. The different conventions of each, while often crossing over into each other, make the argument of a single 'electronic' language a little less persuasive. More appropriate, for these media at least, might be the idea of a series of local dialects, shared by individual communities—albeit virtual ones.

## Email

A comparison of email communications from only a few years ago with some examples from today would be revealing. In their early days emails were largely seen as a direct replacement of posted letters, but sent over an electronic medium. Today's emails tend to be far more conversational and personal. While some remain the electronic equivalent of a traditional letter or memo, sent for speed and convenience, most will dispense with the etiquette of letter writing. So fewer emails today begin with 'Dear'—the preference is clearly for 'Hey', or 'Hi', followed often by a Christian name— and fewer still will use the 'Yours sincerely' or 'Yours faithfully' sign-off. Generally, the shorter the time delay between messages, the less there is a need for a greeting.

While emails do not impose significant space constraints in the same way as text messages do, some of the stylistics of the latter, used for concision, are crossing over. SMS abbreviations (**LOL** for 'lots of love', for example, or **TTFN** for 'ta ta for now'), emoticons such as 'smileys', and other conversational abbreviations such as **bcos**, **v** (for 'very'), and **lotsa**, are all being used in personal email exchanges, and there is a frequent lack of standard capitalization ('went to london today to see buckingham palace'). Even more apparent is the disregard for rules of punctuation and grammar. It is telling that while a traditional letter containing misspellings and ungrammatical sentences would be seen as a reflection of the educational status of the sender, such mistakes in emails are commonly accepted as a more or less inevitable result of the writer's speed and natural thought processes.

Email messages are not, however, a language free-for-all. Some rules do persist, and out of virtually all electronic forums emails remain closest in their conventions to those of traditional letter-writing—their legal status, much debated, is also broadly similar. What does seem clear is that emails are regarded as having distinct linguistic and stylistic characteristics, ranging from the practical, such as the use of witty or eye-catching headings, to the subjective and highly personal.

## Chat groups

If email language is still at a relatively early stage in its evolution, this is even more true of chat-room language, which is developing a lexicon and style of its own at a rapid rate.

Online discussions, carried out in so-called chat 'rooms' and bulletin boards on the Internet, are usually devoted to a single subject or are populated by a particular group—people interested in a particular sports team, for example, or who live in one neighbourhood. Interaction between interested users can take place in real time (known as 'synchronous' conversation), or in delayed time ('asynchronous'). In the first situation, a visitor enters the room and can immediately join in an ongoing, real-time, conversation. In the latter, a visitor can access various postings on a site made over time and either read or add to the conversation as they wish. Some messages are headed so that visitors can click into the responses or opinions (known as a 'thread') they are interested in; these headings are often similar to newspaper headlines in their use of linguistic devices such as punning. It is, however, the real-time conversations which tend to feature the most striking linguistic characteristics.

The etiquette rules of chat rooms can be strict, and a whole series of labels has evolved for participants who choose to adhere to them or to ignore them. **Lurkers** (those who visit a chat room and merely listen in without contributing), **newbies** (newcomers to a chat room, often looked down on by the **leet** or **regs**, the 'elite' or 'regulars'), and **flamers** (people who post deliberately hostile messages), are all categories of chat-room user. Beyond this human lexicon is a distinct chat-room style of 'talking'. The medium encourages personal, and often idiosyncratic, conversation, and language play is common. The use, for example, of nicknames, or **nicks**, is a distinctive feature of real-time chat-group language. In this virtual world, people rarely use their own name, and their personal choices of monikers can be colourful (and sometimes lewd). The choice of a 'nick' is part of a ritual for newbies, who choose their electronic identity for the group they join. These nicknames also play an important role in messages themselves, which do not always imitate real-life conversations in their rhythm of speaking and listening, and which frequently overlap with each other. The result can be confusing, but the use of a nickname in a direct address becomes invaluable in linking exchanges.

Actions or comments on the part of chat-room participants are sometimes introduced by a single asterisk: '*ActionMan is not following the drift', or by double colons '::wink::'. The number of resulting punctuation marks gives a web 'page' of conversation a distinctive look, as does the use of SMS emoticons and other forms of transcription for emotions (including exclamations such as 'euugh' and 'eek'). Repeated punctuation marks, such as !!!!! or ?????, are also often used as expressions in their own right. As in email, abbreviations and elisions are used, but to a far greater extent: the need for speed means that the replacement of **r** for 'are' and **b** for 'be' are the norm, as are **prolly** for 'probably' and **peeps** for 'people'. Frequently, words are joined together to form whole strings of uninterrupted compounds: 'he's a realkissmyasskindaguy', an effect also achieved by strings of words with little punctuation or division. The use of 'fillers' such as **innit** and **like** are commonplace.

The use of **leetspeak** (discussed on pages 59–60), and other codes such as **rot13**, which replaces each English letter with the one thirteen letters forward or back along the alphabet, are extreme reflections of the type of highly personalized vocabularies sometimes adopted by individual chat groups. Within the 'rot13' system, for example, often used to hide controversial or offensive content, **jbex** means 'work', and traditional inflections are then added as in **jbexing** for 'working' and **jbexed** for 'worked'. Just as slang marks out the territory of a particular gang or group, so chat-room communities have their own argot which affirms group identity and which also disguises information from the uninitiated.

# Blogging

A weblog, or **blog,** is a form of online journal, a personal website on which an individual or group of users record their opinions on a regular basis. The relatively simple act of creating one immediately introduces a whole lexicon of terms playing on those four letters. Updating your blog makes you part of the **blogosphere** (the set of all blogs), while the reference to other blogs on your site is known as a **blogroll** (like 'logrolling'). Words can be posted on a **personalblog, friendblog,** or a **travelblog.** A blog which includes photos with comments is a **photoblog,** one with video footage is a **vlog,** while one with comic strips is termed a **stripblog.** Blogging from an event is known as **liveblogging.** Finally, content can be uploaded directly from your mobile phone in a process known as **moblogging.** Not all blogs are called such—sometimes they are referred to simply as journals (especially if created using the popular site *LiveJournal*).

Participants in blogs may meet up **IRL** (in real life) or may stay as purely a **netfriend** or **keypal.** In both cases, the site moves closer to becoming an 'online social network', typified particularly by the frenzied growth of *Friendster,* a site dedicated purely to increasing one's list of friends-of-friends-of-friends. The notion of friendship within blogs is a complex and fairly loaded one, perhaps an inevitability given the intimate nature of what is essentially a personal journal. If a regular visitor removes themselves from a list of friends they are what is called **unfriending,** an action regretted by the keeper of the blog unless that visitor is a **scrial adder,** namely someone who befriends many users at once.

The linguistic nature of blogs is not as distinctive as that of emails, texts, or chat-room postings. It is heavily influenced by the styles and terms of the latter which have wandered over, and the use of SMS language in particular is very common. Some less usual words have however also become common in blogs: **meme,** based on the scientific use of the term denoting something that is self-propagating, is a word much used as people fill up their posts with ideas borrowed from other people and given a vaguely personal twist, for example a top one hundred films list, posted with a blogger's own additions. For the most part, however, blogs are not written in an exclusive way—the philosophy of the blogging community is that anyone can write them and anyone can understand them.

# SMS (short message system)

According to one mobile-phone operator, by the end of the next decade over half of the world's population will be using mobile phones. The effect of this on our language, lamented by many who see a decline in linguistic and grammatical values as inevitable, is likely to be significant. Today's children have been called 'the thumb generation'.

SMS language is necessarily the most abbreviated form of communication—most mobile-phone networks restrict users to around 160 characters per message. This space constraint accounts for the highly abbreviated form of words used, as well as the translation of emotions into the symbols known as emoticons. From this beginning, however, has grown a highly colourful, witty, and idiosyncratic vocabulary which is continually evolving. While emoticons look to be on the decline, new forms of text language are emerging. Capital letters are being given syllabic value, as in **nEd** for 'need', and **thN** for 'then', while single characters are becoming more common, so **Z**, for example, is now often used for 'said'. Non-alphabet characters are also starting to be used: **c%l** for 'cool', for example. Multi-word expressions, particularly of a stereotyped kind, continue to be reduced to a string of capital letters, as in **YYSW** for 'yeah, yeah, sure, whatever'.

Text messaging is never far from the news, and in some cases makes front-page headlines. In 2004, the British paper *News of the World* published an alleged text exchange between footballer David Beckham and Rebecca Loos. Newspaper readers across Britain tried to fill in the blanks in the censored, asterisk-laden messages. Earlier in the same year, the moves announced by several British companies again underscored the absorption of text messaging into the very fabric of our lives. One of these, British Gas, formally encouraged its staff to use abbreviated text language in memos, emails, and even on the phone as a venture to save it thousands of pounds each year. The glossary sent out to employees included **:) BG Cuz** (happy British Gas customer), and **Cuz F2T 2day** (customer is free to talk today).

# MUD games

**MUD** games (a term standing for 'Multi-User Dungeon' games and now denoting virtual role-playing games in general), have also developed their own unique ways of communicating. Within 'MUDs', fantasy worlds are created which are inhabited by mythical beings such as elves, goblins, and sorcerers. The goal of the game is to slay monsters and to complete quests. Alongside MUDs are MUSHes (for 'Multi-User Shared Hallucinations'): online fantasy worlds to which multiple users are connected at the same time, **MUCK**s (for 'Multi-User Chat Kingdoms', in which the game's emphasis is on player interaction), and a host of other **MMORPG**s ('Massive Multi-Player Online Role-Playing Games'). Fanatics of another MUD variant known as a **talker**—one which has most of its complex bits of code stripped away, leaving just the communication commands—are known as **spods** (as opposed to 'ordinary' **mudders**). A get-together of computer games fans (themselves known as **LARPers**—Live Action Role-Players) is sometimes called a **LAN party** (for 'local area network party').

Each of the above virtual worlds provides evidence of the potential for linguistic creativity within individual 'speech' communities. The conventions used may depart radically from what we know as standard English, but their influence on current language is only likely to increase. The result may be far from a homogeneous language; rather we may see a series of highly individual languages which, even as they brush up against each other, provide strong markers of identity for the communities they serve.

# 11

# Boos, Babes, and Cribs:
## The New Street Slang

**Slang is a language that rolls up its sleeves, spits on its hands and goes to work.**
Poet and author Carl Sandburg, writing in the *New York Times*.

**Slang is a linguistic luxury, it is a sport, and like any other sport, something that belongs essentially to the young.**
Danish linguist Otto Jespersen, in *Mankind, Nation, and Individual*, 1946.

**Grunting teenagers face tests in talking.**
Headline in the *Daily Mail*, February 2004.

**Correct English is the slang of prigs who write history and essays.**
George Eliot.

We have long accepted that language is always in flux, but it is less obvious that some parts of it move more quickly than others. The rate of change is entirely dictated by our, the users', needs, and few things illustrate this better than slang, which has one of the fastest turnover rates of words and meanings of any area in language—so fast, in fact, that by the time it is recorded it might already be gone.

The vocabulary used by a group is as key a factor in its identity as any demarcations of age, social status, race, or the hundreds of other factors with which we define ourselves. One of the best means we have of staking out our territory is our vocabulary, a tribal brand which speaks as loudly as the latest fashion item or consumer desirable. Slang is typically the vocabulary of a particular group, used by speakers as a kind of badge of inclusiveness as well as a means of excluding those (such as parents) outside the circle. In Britain, the distinct groups which make up its subculture have created their own unique vocabularies, so that Burberry-clad 'townies' (urban-dwelling teenagers who wear upmarket garb) do linguistic battle with the alternative 'grungers' and 'skaters', 'neds' and 'chavs' (see pages 45–46). Moreover, the power slang holds to articulate identity is growing: the opportunities for new words to take root are vastly increased by new media such as the Internet and text messaging.

The evolution of new meanings is usually so discreet that we rarely give much thought to their heritage. This is not the case with slang, which wears the intentions of its creators on its metaphorical sleeve. From **wicked** of the 1980s to **tight** in the early years of this century, teenage slang intentionally takes older words and gives them new meanings, a kind of language 'subversiveness' which becomes a marker of attitude and rebellion. Rap music and black slang (**Blinglish**) have been particularly strong forces in remoulding vocabulary to create something new and highly individual—so much so that in March 2004 a school in Sheffield announced that it was adopting a new concept in teaching English, in which classical texts would be compared to hip-hop lyrics. The initiative is part of a wider move to improve the literacy skills of schoolchildren by bringing slang into the classroom. It will be fascinating to see whether the act of pulling into the mainstream a language which thrives on its difference will diminish its power.

Slang has always existed. What is new is the way in which it is entering the written media—in texting, chat rooms, and in emails—and the jury is out as to whether it is having a newly detrimental effect on our writing skills. Yet even if it is looked down upon by prescriptivists and devotees of 'correct' English, slang will always break through; its importance may even grow as overground and underground cultures continue to come together. It is also incontestably an area which displays enormous creativity. Perhaps American educator and US senator Samuel I. Hayakawa expressed it most simply when he wrote that 'slang is the poetry of everyday life'.

**anything:** nothing special, as in *'that skirt is anything'*.

**bodyswerve:** to give something a miss; to avoid something. The term was first used in sport, and the first recorded example of extended use as a   69

noun, according to the *Oxford English Dictionary*, was in 1984. The
related verb to **swerve** means to avoid plans at the last minute.

**big up:** to recommend something highly; to talk something or someone
up. **Big up!** is also used as an expression meaning 'well done!', and as a
cooler equivalent of 'Hey' or 'Hi'.
I need to let you know that when I put word out that I was going to interview you,
women sent emails bigging you up and saying to tell you that they love you.
Interview with dance-hall singer Lady Saw in *www.jouvay.com*.

**blato** (abbreviation): blatantly. The term is often used sarcastically and
at the end of a sentence. **Well blato potato** is a sarcastic response to
something obvious which doesn't need saying.

## Behind the bling

Despite being recorded in print for the first time in 1999, **bling-
bling** (or simply **bling**) could with some justification be called the
defining word of the early 'noughties'. It is journalists' favourite way
of summing up our supposedly over-materialistic, celebrity-
obsessed society at the beginning of the twenty-first century, much
as Harry Enfield's catchphrase 'Loadsamoney!' remains popular
British shorthand for the booming Thatcherite eighties, and just as
'stealth wealth' was a term of the nineties.

Used to refer to ostentatiously expensive clothing or jewellery, or
the style or attitudes associated with them, 'bling-bling' was
probably suggested by the idea of light reflecting off a diamond, or
the sound of jewellery clashing together. It first appeared as a song
title by US rapper B.G. ('Baby Gangsta') in 1999, since when it has
moved out of the hip-hop world and into the mainstream in Britain
as well as America, acquiring along the way a bewildering range of
variants and uses.

'Bling' now functions as a noun, an adjective, and a verb, and has
generated numerous spin-off words such as **bling-blingy**, **un-bling**,
and **blinger**. In each of these it denotes something vulgar and
showy. While its time will pass (**post-bling** is already being used),

and a new word will emerge to sum up the next big social trend, 'bling-bling' will probably live on as a term that instantly evokes the early 2000s.

**It don't mean a thing if it ain't got that bling-bling.**
*Rolling Stone*, 2000.

**There is a new Hollywood 'It' girl and she's as far from bling as they come.**
*B*, 2003.

**Guys in charge of huge corporations bling-blinged all through the 1990s.**
*New York Times*, 2003.

**Elvis was the first white boy to really bling it up.**
*New York Times*, 2003.

**Check your bling-blingy accoutrements at the door.**
*New York* magazine, 2001.

**Post-bling is different—far more dandyish than stealth wealth, but far less vulgar than bling-bling.**
*The Guardian*, 2004.

**boo:** girlfriend or boyfriend, used in similar ways to 'baby' or 'honey'.

**chirps:** to flirt with; to chat up.
**P Diddy is still trying to chirps J-Lo!**
Headline on *www.rwdmag.com*, February 2004.

**beanie:** a pretty girl.

**bongoed:** drunk; stoned. The term may have its origin in the word 'bong', meaning a pipe used for smoking cannabis.
**So, back at the hotel, I carry on. I don't know how many grams I did, but it was an easy ten. I was bongoed.**
*Front* magazine, 2003.

**butters:** ugly (a shortening of 'butt ugly').

**babylicious:** very attractive. The adjective is a variation on the more established **bootylicious**, which has the same meaning.
**Spritz onto damp locks and scrunch dry. Baby-licious!**
> *Sugar* magazine, August 2003.

**crib:** home. The term was originally a nineteenth-century slang term among thieves, recorded from 1819 in the *Oxford English Dictionary*, and used particularly in the phrase *crack a crib*, meaning to break into a house. It then went underground but has recently re-emerged in US slang.
**Hey babe, wanna come over to my crib?**
> Internet discussion site, March 2004.

**coinkydinky** (pronounced co-inkydinky): coincidence. The term is a humorous play on the original word.
**A car pulls up. Fancy. Same kind that was here before but not. That's whatcha call a co-inky-dinky.**
> Suzan-Lori Parks, *Getting Mother's Body: A Novel* , 2003.

**g-fab:** a contraction of 'ghetto fabulous', meaning glamorous in an over-the-top way. The term was originally hip-hop slang and is very similar to the adjective 'bling-bling'.

**grimy:** great; a term of approval.

**pash:** a kiss. A **pash rash** is sore lips resulting from a lot of kissing, while **pash and dash** is the kissing of a stranger, usually while drunk. The term originates in Australian and New Zealand slang, and is a contraction of 'passion'.
**The guy I pashed was really cute man and he told me his name was Kennedy which is such a lie and I found out that his real name was Kent. OK girls find out the true facts about the boy you're pashing before you really pash him.**
> *nzgirl.co.nz*, 2004.

**shroomer:** a person who uses hallucinogenic ('magic') mushrooms to get their kicks. 'Shroomer' comes from *shroom*, short for mushroom, and is first recorded in US sources in the 1980s. In a more innocent vein, 'shroomer' can also be used to describe a person who gathers wild mushrooms for food. The term is one of the more recent in a whole line of informal terms for users of illegal drugs, from **baseheads** and **junkies** to **stoners** and **schmeckers**.

**pikey** (offensive): scruffy, or ill-bred. The term, which is used both as a noun and an adjective, was originally a racially offensive term for a gypsy. In its more recent, transferred, sense, it is used as a more general (though still offensive) term for someone considered to be inferior or lower-class. **Reebok Classics—you cannot claim any Geezer status without these—must be gleaming white, gold stripes are best . . . yellow or orange are considered a bit pikey by the Geezer hierarchy.**
'How to be A Geezer', *www.eryc.co.uk* (UK Skateboard Community).

**sleb:** short for 'celebrity'.

**solid:** a term of approval for something or somebody good.

**what's crackalackin?:** used as a general greeting, similar to 'what's up?' or 'what's new?'.
**What's poppin' wit'chu? What's happenin'? What's crackalackin'?**
Extract from Aceyalone's *Let me Hear some Lyrics*.

## Shibby

The term **shibby** has become a multi-purpose slang word. It has a whole variety of positive meanings, depending on context. The term was introduced in the 2001 movie entitled *Dude, where's my car?* in which 'shibby' is used numerous times in many different guises. Originally used to describe drugs such as marijuana, it was neutralized to mean 'cool' after the film's classification was changed to allow children to see it and drug references were taken out.

As an adjective, 'shibby' means positive, pleasing, or successful, and can also be used as a single-word response meaning 'cool'.

As a noun, 'shibby' can be a nickname for a lover, as well as a fun replacement for almost any noun (*He wrote me a shibby bout shibby*).

As a verb, the word can mean to understand (*do you shibby?*), to engage in sexual intercourse (*I want to shibby you right now*), or to play or waste time (*let's cut with the shibbying and get on*).

A 2003 analysis of the term by *The Observer* neatly captures the broad spectrum of uses to which 'shibby' can be put:
One may coo 'shibby' or 'He's shibby' when someone attractive walks by, or constantly exclaim 'shibby' in the company of shibby friends. Some, wrapped up in the pleasure and pride of the word, now refer to their erection as their shibby, to making love as shibby, to their lover as their shibby, or else their weed/dope or bong as shibby.

# 12

# Keeping Their Word:
## The Language of Brands

**Words can have no single fixed meaning. No one owns them or has a proprietary right to dictate how they will be used.**
> Poet and critic David Lehman, *Sign of the Times*.

**Dr. Pierce's Pleasant Pellets for the Liver Makes Weak Women Strong, Sick Women Well by giving Strength to the Stomach, Purity to the Blood and Life to Lungs.**
> Advertisement in the *Cambridge Jeffersonian*, 1904.

**Liza . . . applies her blusher in a long Nike tick, which extends right up to her ear to give her the most incredible cheekbones.**
> *Marie Claire* magazine, 2003.

**The new names are always Latin. That is another reason why people think it's bollocks.**
> Professor Deborah Cameron on the contractor Jarvis' changing of its name to 'Engenda', 2004.

On 1 April 2004 a new radio station for London gave its first broadcast. Despite its launch date, FCUK FM, broadcast from the clothes chain French Connection's flagship store in London's Regent Street, was not a joke—rather it was meant as a serious challenge to mainstream radio and as a sensational piece of branding. The station included adverts for things that can't be bought, such as patience, time, sleep, and honesty. This virtual advertising stood alongside French Connection's very real and commercial branding exercise, the subject of much controversy since its beginning. The bedrock of the company's campaign is a single abbreviation, **fcuk**, a rearrangement of the expletive 'fuck'. The 'fcuk' phenomenon is fascinating evidence of the possible permutations on a single word, greater even than those in another celebrated campaign, for the mineral water Perrier, which also relied on language play with its slogans **H2eau, Heau, Heau, Heau** (at Christmas time), and **Eau Dear** (when England was knocked out of the World Cup). French Connection's device may have greater staying power. First aired in 1996, the fcuk concept has spiralled. Recent slogans include **Guaranteed fcuk**, **What the fcuk**, **Fcukiki summer**, and **My place now fcuk**. Parodies of the campaign have been rife, including one from a disgruntled *Guardian* columnist living close to a French Connection store, in an article entitled 'When your neighbours scuk'.

The appropriation of language by companies in their advertising campaigns brings into question the whole notion of language ownership. While the Nike tick or 'swoosh' is now a brand of a visual kind, forever associated with its creators, there is also a linguistic category of phrases which have been more or less taken over by companies through their advertising. **Va va voom**, a slogan for Renault cars, has been a figurative term since the 1950s, denoting 'oomph' or sex appeal. Its use today is frequently in either tacit or explicit reference to the ads and to cars.

Conversely, words such as 'hoover', 'elevator', 'thermos', 'aspirin', and 'kleenex' were previously trademarked but have now become generic items of vocabulary. Similarly, some slogans are absorbed into general language to the extent that their origins, however colourful, become lost. Few viewers of the 1980s British TV series *Only Fools and Horses*, or of celebrity-chef Jamie Oliver's programmes, would know that the phrase **luvvly jubbly** evolved from an orange drink of the same name from the fifties, 'jubbly'. The term has today lost all its proprietary force.

There is another category of advertising language in which simple, non-fixed phrases become recognizable and thus 'fixed', bringing something to a word or phrase which wasn't there before: in other words, they are successful slogans. One such phrase to enter the mainstream comes from a campaign conducted by the US telephone company Verizon, a major

supplier of mobile phones. Their ad, drawing on the fact that there are vast areas in the US where a good phone signal is hard to find, features a geeky-looking technician in all sorts of venues, walking about and every few seconds saying into his cellphone **Can you hear me now?** in order to test the reliability of the Verizon signal. The phrase 'Can you hear me now?' has rapidly caught on, and has gone far beyond its initial application (one site on the Internet is even captioned 'Can You Kill Me Now?').

A slightly older US slogan is still proving productive. A series of ads, originally made for the California Milk Processing Board and subsequently licensed by the National Dairy Board, features the phrase **Got milk?** The simplicity of the phrase has turned it into a linguistic icon: conscious conversational spin-offs such as 'Got wine?', 'Got junk?', 'Got rice?', are commonplace, as are bumper stickers asking 'Got Jesus?'. In a mountainous area of Colorado where there is a lot of big game hunting, a meat processing plant even asks the question 'Got elk?'. These general uses of the phrase are conscious follow-ups to its original meaning in the ads: the notion that the thing named (milk or whatever) is an essential that you don't want to be without. Extended usages are also appearing, suggesting that at some point the original may well disappear from view: 'Got ripped off?' being one recent example.

Finally, a further example of our adoption of slogans can be found in the 1990s slogan for the wood varnish Ronseal: **It does exactly what it says on the tin**. Recorded in publications as varied as the *Daily Telegraph* and *Muzik* magazine, it means that something or someone does exactly (and no more than) what is expected of them. A recent profile of the actor Jim Carrey offers a good example: 'If his comedy appears to be writ large in bright crayons, each film does exactly what it says on the tin. You can dub him in Japanese, Swahili, Swedish—the chap is cast-iron reliable'. In most cases, silent homage is still paid to the original ad—even in the latest extended uses such as 'does exactly what it says on the box'.

Advertising in these cases is directing language, originating new uses of it. It can also be a powerful disseminator of what is already there. The phrase **big up** has been used in many ads (including one for the cheesy snack Wotsits) and its use neatly reflects the audience that is being aimed at: teenagers, for whom the slang is second nature. Fast-food chain

McDonald's looked to the same teen vernacular for its slogan **I'm loving it**. The latter did not endear itself to language purists, for whom advertising copy is a bête noire. A recent campaign for Norwich Union's car insurance carried the slogan **Let us quote you happy**. The result was cries from many of a crime against language, but for all (perhaps because of?) its ungrammatical construction, the slogan nonetheless lodged itself in the public mind.

<hr>

Branding is far from limited to products. The meaning of the term itself extends a long way beyond its original sense of 'brand name': a brand today is core to the success or failure of an enterprise. Language is a key component in any branding or rebranding exercise, whether for a political party or even a country, as in the recent 'Marke Deutschland' initiative for Germany or New Labour's 'Cool Britannia' branding campaign of the 1990s. One of the most dramatic rebranding tools is the changing of a name. The British high-street favourite Marks & Spencer, affectionately known as simply M&S, dropped its reassuring but rather staid 'St Michael's' label in favour of new sub-brands such as the exotically named 'Per Una' clothing range. Other companies, such as lastminute.com, have used their Internet domain names as their company name, embracing another common trend of using lower-case letters. Both moves are examples of the shift away from simple proper names to those which try to encapsulate a lifestyle or aspirational ideal.

<hr>

Recent years have seen a host of companies look to Latin for their new brands, probably for its ring of tradition. Jarvis, the engineering contractor, adopted 'Engenda', a term which was actually fake Latin and which attracted a fair amount of derision (as did, rather inevitably, the name 'Arriva' for a British train operator). The Royal Mail caused an outcry when it chose the name 'Consignia' (also fake Latin), a decision which was subsequently and rapidly overturned. Other companies trod the same path: British Steel became 'Corus', the insurance company Norwich Union chose 'Aviva', and the MSF trade union adopted 'Amicus'. Departing from this trend was the announcement in 2004 by the train company Eurostar that it plans to change the name of London's St Pancras rail terminal to something more straightforward: its current name is thought to be too obscure to foreign travellers who will begin arriving there in 2007.

The extent to which language can be owned is debatable. No trademark can prevent a phrase or slogan from entering the mainstream if it is successful enough. While the name of search engine Google is protected from competitors, the verb 'google' has quickly become a generic term for online searching, and carries no trademark designation. Equally, few examples of 'branded' language stand the test of time. Even the enormous impact of the reality TV show *'I'm a Celebrity . . . Get Me Out of Here!'*, whose title has found its way into hundreds of different contexts and extended uses, wanes fairly quickly when off air. Ultimately, language continually proves itself to be bigger than brands.

# 13

# So Not Liking That:
## Grammatical Grievances

**Usage is the only test. I prefer a phrase that is easy and unaffected to a phrase that is grammatical.**
British writer W. Somerset Maugham, in his *Writer's Notebook*.

**I'm deeply touched by that warm and generous welcome. That's more than I deserve and more than I'm used to, quite frankly.**

**The idea that people around that table . . . would want to give it all away is, quite frankly, a bit dumb.**
Tony Blair in a speech to the US Congress, July 2003, and on the eve of an EU summit in Brussels, 2004, demonstrating his fondness for the filler 'quite frankly'.

If English is seen by many as a language in decline, then grammar, or its misuse, is the area most often held up as proof. Rather like punctuation, the conventions of grammar are not as inflexible as we may assume, and they evolve just as surely as our vocabulary. Changes of usage, however, will not suit everyone, and every age has had its controversies; if today we lament the adverbial *like*, used so frequently that it has begun to function as a form of punctuation, the purists of the sixteenth century insisted that Shakespeare's *laughable* ought to be changed to *laugh-at-able*, while the eighteenth-century heard many a debate over the distinction between *shall* and *will*, and *different from* and *different to*. There are hundreds of such examples (among which perhaps the most famous is the contentious 'split infinitive') which demonstrate that changes in grammar are as continuous and inevitable as those in our vocabulary. Moreover, just as words from the past are resurrected as we need them, so grammatical changes can come full circle: the use of *their* as a singular possessive to mean 'his or her' has been in use since at least the sixteenth century, while the controversial use of *disinterested* to mean 'uninterested' (as opposed to 'impartial') is in fact the earliest recorded use of the word.

## Filling time

In a 2004 poll published by the Plain English Commission (an independent body which gives accreditation to clear and straightforward language use in the literature of professional and commercial institutions, including government), the use of the word *like* as a 'filler' in sentences was voted one of the top ten linguistic bugbears of the British public. 'Fillers' are words used frequently in certain slots in dialogue or prose without contributing significantly to the meaning. *Totally, like,* and *innit* are all fillers, as are more traditional examples such as *well, sort of,* and *you know.*

*Like* in this modern sense came into prominence with 'Valley Girl' speak (and famously in Frank and Moon Unit Zappa's 1982 song *Valley Girl,* as well as in US films such as *Clueless*). Valley Girls were not, however, the first to use it in this way. Jazz musicians and beat poets used it as a filler word as early as the 1950s, while in the late 1970s 'like' began to be used to introduce a thought or related speech. Today, its popularity is such that it has also infiltrated the speech of older generations. Like many such fillers, it has a growing number of applications. It can tell the listener that what is being said is an approximation (and often an exaggeration), as in *He has, like, a zillion CDs,* or be used for emphasis to demonstrate that the piece of information that follows is important: *She is, like, so babelustic.* The practice of using it to introduce reported speech has also become increasingly popular: *She'd say 'I went crazy last night!' and I'm like, 'Oooh, what'd you do?'* (*Premiere* magazine, 2001.)

Defenders of 'fillers', such as psycholinguists, argue that such usages are a natural evolution of language. They see words such as 'like' as having a highly useful function, giving a speaker time to gather their thoughts. Some studies, including one by US linguists Susan Brennan and Michael Shober, even suggest that people who have been taught not to use filler words are interrupted more often. Fillers are, in other words, exploitable resources rather than simple throwaways.

The use of fillers can be of great parodic value. Oxford's reading programme suggests that they are being used increasingly, and effectively, as a method of caricature: *Don't you have, like, a dishwasher? Like, my foot's getting tired pumping water. I never have to, like, scrub pans at home* (*Canadian Yachting*, 2000). For impressionists such as the British Rory Bremner, fillers can be an ideal means of characterization. Bremner liberally scatters *quite frankly* throughout his take-off of Tony Blair, while the British PM's *y'know*, described by many as an attempt to get onside with his voters by using so-called 'Estuary English', has also been the object of some parody.

*Innit*, meanwhile, is a term on the move, and new uses are still evolving. Originally a simple contraction of 'isn't it?' at the end of a sentence (*It's cold today, innit?*), the term has gone on to develop into an all-purpose filler, often used in unsyntactical ways: *I'm just separating the sheep from the goats, Claz, the sheep from the goats. That's Matthew. And I think you yourself are a sheep, innit?* (Zadie Smith, *White Teeth*, 2000). Most recently, *innit* is now also used without any explicit question mark, as a general-purpose filler used primarily for emphasis and confirmation: *I bought that choon back in 1998 with my cousin, innit, and we been lickin' it ever since. True say.* (*Snoop*, 2003). This latest use is especially frequent among young black and Asian communities.

## Umming and erring: verbal white noise?

The latest products using speech-recognition software—computer programs which interpret and understand natural speech by recognizing syntax as well as meaning—are being adapted to accept speech 'disfluencies' as an integral part of the way we speak. There may, it seems, be more to 'uh' and 'um', than first appears.

Once seen as a sign of nervousness, or of an ignorance of the subject in hand, linguists are now looking for the actual meaning in words such as 'uh', 'er', and 'um'. The latest—and perhaps most controversial—idea comes from Herbert Clark, a psychologist at Stanford, and Jean Fox Tree, a psycholinguist at the University of California, Santa Cruz, who argue that speakers use (and listeners understand) fillers such as 'uh' and 'um' in distinct ways. 'Uh', they maintain, signals a forthcoming pause which will be short, while 'um' signals a longer pause. Other studies have shown that listeners process speech more quickly with the 'ums' and 'uhs' left in than when they are taken out. As such they become rightful communicators in themselves and have an important function when we speak.

Rather than being seen as an 'acoustic accident', 'um' and 'uh' may yet be acknowledged as active, perhaps even desirable, components of our linguistic repertoire.

## Swapping tenses

Traditionally, in standard English grammar, verbs of 'state' such as 'be', 'like', 'seem', etc. are used only with the standard present tense (called the present indicative), and are not used with the present continuous tense ('this seems fine', not 'this is seeming fine'). Today, however, the verb 'like' is being used informally in the present continuous tense, appearing frequently in weblogs and chat rooms. It is a frequent device of self-parody: *I am so not liking that* is, more often than not, used self-consciously to add a degree of emphasis to the level of dislike. At the same time, however, *I'm liking that* is used without irony, and examples of use are in plentiful supply, even if it has yet to make the leap into more formal contexts. Most recently, past events are being related in the present tense.

## Literally speaking

There is another category of words which behave rather like fillers, but which have a different function, used for emphasis or for reinforcing the adjective which follows them. Current and popular examples of these 'intensifiers' are *well* and *literally*. *My new site is well grimy!* and *I mean literally like you were gone a week*, are two of the hundreds of examples to be found in recent weblog entries.

# Grammatical brouhahas

When the Education Secretary Charles Clarke spoke of 'less people' on the *Today* programme when speaking of raising the standard of communication skills among British schoolchildren, the phone lines of Radio 4 lit up. Clarke came under attack not for his government's policies, but for his use of 'less' rather than 'fewer' when referring to a plural noun. What hope for school standards, the programme listeners complained, if the minister in charge of the education of Britain's schoolchildren could make such a basic grammatical mistake? In fact, the Secretary was making one of the most frequent errors made by native speakers of English ('fewer' is the correct form when denoting a plural).

Controversial or dubious grammatical practices are not limited to public life in Britain. In the US, one fracas broke rather spectacularly into the media in 2003. The debate began with the following sentence:

**Toni Morrison's genius enables her to create novels that arise from and express the injustices African Americans have endured.**

The sentence, which appeared in a scholastic-achievement test taken by college-bound high-school students, became the subject of intense debate when a high-school teacher insisted it was ungrammatical. The objection, which was then echoed by other language purists, was that the antecedent of 'her' in the sentence was 'Toni Morrison's genius', a grammatical error because 'her' could not have, as an antecedent, a noun in the possessive case. The objection was not about whether the sentence was clear—anyone reading it would understand that 'her' really referred to 'Toni Morrison'— but whether the sentence was correct. Following numerous exchanges between the teacher and the testing company, and an attempt to vet the question by an outside panel of experts, the testing company conceded defeat and threw out the question, thereby raising the test scores of any students who had answered it incorrectly. (The students' only task was to indicate whether the sentence was grammatical or not.) The decision was seen by many as a victory of hyper-correctness over common sense.

# 14

# Patterns of Punctuation

I think we're looking at detailed semantics. We are looking at what's a semicolon, what's a dash, what's a full stop.

> The BBC's political editor Andrew Marr on debates over the Government's alleged exaggeration of the threat posed by Iraq in 2003.

Give a civil servant a good case and he'll wreck it with clichés, bad punctuation, double negatives, & convoluted apology.

> The late MP Alan Clark, in his published diaries, 22 July 1983.

The most important part of the title is the comma. Because it seems to me that I am that comma.

> Salman Rushdie, explaining the title of his book *East, West*, August 1994.

There were 50,000 hostile voices and Horrocks went one way, Taylor went the other, and I was left holding his bloody hyphen.

> Rugby player Mick English reported in the *Sunday Times* 2 September 1990, on J. P. Horrocks-Taylor slipping English's tackle to score.

He once telephoned a semicolon from Moscow.

> James Bone, on being asked whether his fellow journalist George Mair had been a fastidious worker.

It would be easy to assume that our interest in punctuation follows a fairly flat graph, with occasional peaks when an example of flagrant misuse touches a nerve. Most of us have our personal bêtes noires, but the overall picture of changing punctuation patterns has rarely been within view. In 2003, the subject came sensationally into the spotlight with the publication of Lynne Truss's *Eats, Shoots & Leaves: The Zero Tolerance Approach to Punctuation.* The book, which takes a cheery look at the rules and why we need them, shot to Number One in best-seller lists throughout the English-speaking world, proving that, if not a nation of pedants, many of us care quite deeply about the state of our language.

If we dig below the surface, Truss's success is perhaps not so surprising. The misuse of language has long been one of the favourite subjects of debate among journalists, and radio hosts often maintain that language issues elicit more phone calls from the public than almost any other. The interest in a book by someone who cares passionately about punctuation is simply further, if dramatic, evidence that many people long for the linguistic equivalent of 'firm government'. If language is a minefield, then it is reassuring to be told what to do. More puzzling then, on the surface, is that so many sacred punctuation rules are currently being flouted, even as we claim to cherish them. Is correct punctuation on the decline, as the colourful examples in Truss's book would suggest and as her reviewers have rushed to argue?

In fact, the age of perfect punctuation has never existed. Until the development of printing in the fifteenth and sixteenth centuries the practice of punctuation was haphazard and unreliable, and today's conventions are infinitely more rigorous than those of the past. Those who cling to a golden age, when 'rules were rules', are perhaps forgetting that history can provide examples of dubious punctuation as controversial as any today. Although punctuated differently by modern editors, Shakespeare's 'to be, or not to be, that is the question' could be taken (probably wrongly) as a prime example of a 'comma splice' in which a comma links two grammatically unrelated clauses. Even pedants can be wrong-footed by the passage of time. Tennyson actually wrote 'Their's not to reason why'—today we would write 'theirs'.

Nor has punctuation slipped off today's educational agenda. In the UK, teaching of the rules of grammar and punctuation has returned to a level of formality not seen for decades, thanks to the focus of the national curriculum. Moreover, it is inevitably the errors in punctuation that trip us up, and not the hundreds of examples of correct use that we encounter every day.

To insist on the robustness of punctuation is not to deny that it is changing, in some cases fundamentally. Some of the most recent trends are heavily influenced by SMS (short message system) and chat-room language, in which dashes are replacing colons, and full stops are being used in the middle of sentences—all reflecting the immediacy of the user's thought processes as they write. To re-evaluate our rules, however, is not to question the need for punctuation altogether: we are simply replacing one convention with another. As long as we communicate in writing—through whichever medium—we will need to punctuate if we are to get our message across.

## Cutting a dash

The replacement of the colon with a dash is one of the biggest bugbears of the punctuation purists. The colon has long been the preserve of more formal print rather than general writing, and the shift towards the dash reflects the increasingly conversational nature of our written words. Just as the vocabulary of SMS messages and chat rooms is creeping across into emails, and even into informal letters, so their punctuation patterns are also entering other written contexts; the dash is just one manifestation of this.

The colon is also frequently (and incorrectly) being replaced by a comma— again a reflection of speech patterns. Examples such as 'I like swimming very much, I go to the pool every week' are now commonplace, whereas strictly correct punctuation would require 'I like swimming very much: I go to the pool every week'.

The semicolon, meanwhile, also looks to be on the decline, and unlike the colon may not be replaced. The move away from complex structures towards shorter statements diminishes the usefulness of a device used to organize lengthy sentences. The semicolon is also often avoided out of doubt over its correct use.

Quantifying scientifically the decrease in the use of the semicolon is problematic given the enormous amount of written material existing today compared with even ten years ago, and the different media available now. It is clear that the semicolon is used infrequently on the Internet, but this medium did not exist before, and the level of informality it invites is entirely new. The same applies to chat-room, email, and text-message language. It is hard to judge whether the lack of the semicolon in informal media will ultimately affect more formal writing. Many predict that it will.

## Apostrophe catastrophes

The apostrophe, and its misuse, seems to provoke more impassioned discussion than any other form of punctuation. The 'Apostrophe Protection Society' was set up to protect the device from those who would, as the society sees it, bring about its ruin, and in Lynne Truss the society has found its (unprofessed) champion. As with full stops and hyphens, apostrophes are being used differently rather than facing extinction. While many of these uses are ungrammatical, the history of the apostrophe has always included contraventions of the rules, including that of 'the greengrocer's apostrophe'—the insertion of an apostrophe in noun plurals such as *apple's* and *pear's*.

The principal role of the apostrophe is to indicate possession (as in *Charlotte's house*).

Its second main function is to show the omission of letters in the contraction of two words into one, such as *I'm*, *he's*, etc. Possessive pronouns do not require apostrophes (*hers*, *yours*, *its*, *ours*, *theirs*). The film *Two Weeks Notice* was for some more notable for its missing apostrophe (it should have read *Weeks'*) than for its box-office stars, while others (including Lynne Truss, who described it as 'a significant milestone on the way to punctuation anarchy') lamented the redundant apostrophe inserted into the name of the pop group 'Hear'Say'.

# One word or two?

If the apparent decline of the apostrophe is a cause of regret for many, the more obvious—and certainly more trackable—disappearance of the hyphen is lamented by few. The ways in which compound words and phrases are written have changed significantly over recent years. So **website** is now preferred to **web-site**, and **air raid** to **air-raid**. In US English, there is a preference for making a single word, while in British English the trend is to keep two separate words: **buck tooth**, for example, tends to be the commonest form in British English, and **bucktooth** the commonest in US English.

The most recent evolutionary stage of the hyphen is not, however, exclusively one of decline. If it has disappeared from many noun compounds, it has conversely started to appear (incorrectly) in phrasal verbs such as **top up**, so that encounters such as *Time to top-up your mobile* (instead of *Time to top up your mobile*) are on the increase. There are signs of a further step in this direction, with phrasal verbs being written as one word, e.g. *They even let me takeaway* (rather than *take away*) *a bottle of sake*. This is still far from being regarded as correct English, but the writing of compound verbal expressions as one word is, it seems, on the rise, and could well move into the mainstream.

Beyond those potential single words of the future are some cases which are already quite established: **anytime, anymore, insofar**, and **underway** are all allowed in Oxford dictionaries as variant spellings of **any time, any more, in so far**, and **under way**. Once again the trend can be tracked in Internet chat rooms. There are hundreds of instances of two words becoming one, most of which are most definitely not standard English. Nonetheless, they are interesting as indicators of what may yet come, so **abit, afterall, allsorts, alot, everytime, infact, inspiteof, upto**, and **nevermind** are all standard turns of phrase in chat-room lexicons. (This spelling of 'nevermind' may well be influenced by the fact that *Nevermind* is the title of the second album by the group Nirvana, released in 1991.)

## Alive and kicking: !!!

A recent example of creative punctuation provides an antidote to prophecies of its impending extinction.

The band !!! chose its name, according to its website, 'because it reflects the excitement shared by the band members, mixed with an intense desire to shake things up'. The band has tried to overcome the dilemma of how to refer to it by suggesting that its name can be pronounced as 'any three repetitive sounds'; their own choices include 'Pow-pow-pow' and 'Chick-chick-chick'.

!!! are not the first to choose a symbol for their name. In 1993, the pop star Prince changed his name to the emblem which had appeared on his album covers. Visually, his new 'name' combined the traditional symbols for male and female, along with a stylized horn. Since there was no obvious word for it, he became known as 'symbol' or, most often, 'the pop star formerly known as Prince'. He has since reverted to the original.

## Where we're @

The origins of the @ sign, earlier termed by the *Oxford English Dictionary* the 'commercial a' and more commonly known today as the 'at sign', date back to Latin scriptoria where it was used as an abbreviation of the word 'ad', meaning 'to', 'towards', or 'at'. Although it secured a place on the keyboard of the first typewriter, @ was used infrequently and was almost exclusively restricted to the field of accounting, where it preceded the price at which goods were being sold. The earliest use in English recorded by the *OED* is in sixteenth-century mercantile records in Europe, used to represent units of measure.

The arrival of the Internet, and specifically of web and email addresses, has brought the @ sign dramatically back into view. The architect of its renaissance, the computer engineer Ray Tomlinson, was the first to create an email address, in this first instance to send a message from one

computer to another in the same room. 'I got there first so I got to choose any punctuation I wanted,' Tomlinson told Glen Owen in *The Times*. Incredibly, his story, and with it that of '@', is to be told in a Hollywood film, whose scriptwriter has spoken of his desire to 'explore the power of the contemporary Cartesian dualism: I am @ something, therefore I am something'.

If few would have invested a sign which had such gentle beginnings with such philosophical meaning, it appears to be a symbol capable of inspiring others too: restaurants and clubs are using it in their names in an effort to be hip, while in Denmark a 'Golden @' award is given to the best web design of the year.

# 15

# Change or Decay?
## New Pronunciations

It is impossible for an Englishman to open his mouth without making some other
Englishman despise him.
George Bernard Shaw in the preface to Pygmalion, 1916.

Cor, lumme, strike me pink, it's anuvver book abaht class. Naow such fing,
is there?
*The Glasgow Herald*, 1998.

Even the aitchless millionaire, though sometimes he . . . learns a BBC accent,
seldom succeeds in disguising himself as completely as he would like to.
George Orwell in *The Road to Wigan Pier*, 1937.

The pronunciation of any language is as subject to change as its vocabulary
and grammar. As with the development of new words, some pronunciation
changes are effectively new coinages, while others are the result of novel
applications of elements already in use.

The concepts of accent and pronunciation are not exactly the same. Accent
is the overall phonetic aspect of a dialect (i.e. the way the speech sounds),
and is related to social factors: which part of the English-speaking world
the speaker comes from, and also their socio-economic background, age,
and gender. A person with a Scottish accent, for example, sounds the
words *cot* and *caught* identically, while a person from the south of England
says the first with a short o sound and the second with a long *or* sound.
An American accent, on the other hand, sounds the *t* in a word like *butter*
more like a *d* to British ears. A speaker's accent will of course influence the
way they pronounce something, but pronunciation includes other

variations not necessarily connected to accent: the way, for instance, a speaker stresses certain syllables of a word or phrase. Dialect, meanwhile, is a matter of vocabulary as well as accent.

As far as accents go, English has an exceptionally rich range. It was traditionally held that a good deal of information about a speaker's geographic and social origins could be inferred from even the smallest sample of their speech. However, as social structures change and people grow more mobile, this view is ever more open to question. In recent decades, there have been many changes in the accents of British English. The conservative countryside accents elicited for the *Survey of English Dialects* by speaking to *NORMS* (non-mobile older rural males) are declining, while urban varieties are flourishing and changing. A process known as levelling is said to be taking place, whereby local distinctive features are smoothed out, differences between regional varieties are reduced, and new features emerge and are spread over a wider area. The shifting of communities brings with it a naturally imitative process by which people take on additional or different linguistic features.

This loosening of the ties between accent and class is just as evident in our general pronunciation patterns. Today, a teenager's individual style of pronunciation stands as much for their social identity as their class or background. Using *v* for *th* (*my bruvver*), or dropping the *t* sound from *party*, operates as a kind of pronunciation 'slang'—marking out those who use it as members of a certain in-crowd. Adults can use pronunciation in the same way. A neutral voice is no longer the pronunciation of choice in some professions and particularly in radio and television, both of which have seen a fairly dramatic shift from the cut-glass 'BBC' English to 'Mockney' (affected or 'mock' Cockney) in recent times. In professions such as these, more regional pronunciation patterns are often preferred, or selected ones at least: Scottish or Irish accents have high approval rating whereas Birmingham and Liverpool accents are still stigmatized.

## Changes in Received Pronunciation

Received Pronunciation, or RP, is a term used to refer to a particular accent of English, traditionally characteristic of educated speakers from the south-east of England. RP has been a troublesome and imprecise term ever since it was first proposed by phonetician Daniel Jones. In his *English Pronouncing Dictionary* (1917), Jones based the pronunciations on a model which he initially called 'Public School Pronunciation', 'most usually heard in everyday speech in the families of southern English persons whose menfolk have been educated at the great public boarding-schools'. His model was an early version of the continuing British worry of an undue emphasis on the middle and upper classes of the south-east. Despite the narrow nature of Jones's model, and the manifold problems with its precise description, RP has survived as a term for a kind of standard English pronunciation, generally considered to be the correct one.

It would be wrong, however, to regard RP as a linguistic touchstone which means the same thing to all people, or which has not changed over the last century. The changes which have occurred have been carefully charted by sociolinguists. Early changes in RP included a shift in the vowel in *off*, from *aw* as in *law* to *o* as in *lot*; the disappearance of a tapped r in phrases like *very sorry* (try saying it with a quick *d* sound instead of an *r*); the loss of the *y* sound coming after the *s* in *super*; and the opening of the open front vowel in *the cat sat on the mat* from a sound which was closer to the *e* in today's *set* and *met* to a more contemporary *a* sound. Today, this kind of conservative RP is almost never heard except in stereotypical portrayals of formal old-fashioned speech. It is the so-called 'Queen's English', which even the Queen no longer speaks and which survives largely as a means of caricature, as in an issue of *Publishers Weekly* from 1975 which speaks of 'tea from a bone china teapot—veddy British!'.

Other changes have also been observed, changes which RP shares with other varieties of English. These include the emergence of a *ch* sound in place of a *ty*, and a *j* sound in place of a *dy*, in words like *tune* and *duel*, so *Tuesday* becomes *chooseday*, and *duel* becomes indistinguishable from *jewel*, and the insertion of a *p* or *t* in words such as *emphasis* (pronounced as *empfasis*) or *sense* (*sents*). If lamented by conservative RP speakers, who characterize them as incorrect, such changes reflect a normal process of connected speech, similar to the *r* which appears between vowel sounds in *law and order*. It was out of the latter that the character 'Lora Norder' was born: 'Lora Norder has been done to death and, as far as these voters were concerned, the conventional prescriptions, such as locking offenders up, ought to be euthanased' (Graham Young in *On Line Opinion* in 2004 on the New South Wales election in Australia).

One final sound change, which was by the mid-twentieth century
94  becoming acceptable even in RP (if of the non-conservative variety and

only in some contexts), has been the notorious 'glottal stop', as in the words *Scotland* or *football*, in which the normal *t* sound, made by the tongue on the roof of the mouth, is replaced by a closure of the glottis by the vocal folds. This is said to have originated in Scotland, although it is more commonly thought of as being an essential ingredient of Cockney English. Today many people, and particularly the young, use the glottal stop and are extending it to the final *t* in words as well as those in the middle (*it* becomes simply *i*, as in t*ake i off*).

## The latest sounds

The glottal stop is just one in a range of changes to have emerged in recent years. Some of these changes have been associated with so-called 'Estuary English', a newly observed variety of English pronunciation said to be spoken in London and the south-east, and thus identified with the Thames Estuary. In fact its features also occur elsewhere, notably in northern England where many were in evidence long before.

### 'th'

The shift in the pronunciation of *th* in British English is significant. Its sound is replaced with *v* and *f*, depending on whether it is 'voiced', as in *brother*, or unvoiced, as in *thing* (so 'thing' becomes *fing*, 'brother' becomes *bruvver*, and 'bath' becomes *barf*). This phenomenon of what dialectologists call 'Th-fronting' can be traced as far back as the mid-1860s to Yorkshire, and is certainly on the increase today. 'Th' is recognized as one of the last set of phonemes that native English-speaking children master, often not until after they begin school; it is also a sound which many foreign learners of English have difficulty with, given its absence in most other languages (with the exception of Castilian Spanish), and that it is not easily assimilated to another sound—French speakers stereotypically say *z* instead of a voiced *th*, for example.

### 'l'

Another change involves what is known as 'l-vocalization', where the *l* sound in words like *call* and *milk* (the so-called 'dark' *l*, as opposed to the 'light' *l* which occurs in words like *lift*), which comes after vowels, at the end of words, and in consonant clusters, becomes a vowel similar to the *u* vowel in *put*.

# st/sht

A relatively new feature of speech in southern England is the pronunciation of 'st' as 'sht' in words such as *street* and *stupid* (giving *shtreet* and *shtupid*). Although used most frequently by the young, the pattern is also evident in adult speech and even in that of some British newsreaders.

# Stress

Consider which syllable of these English words you would stress. In each case, there are at least two possible answers.

> **kilometre**
> **controversy**
> **dispute**
> **cervical**
> **research**

# Answers

### kilometre

KILL-o-meet-uhr or kil-OM-uh-tuhr? The former is preferred by some, partly because it follows the pattern of centimetre and millimetre; but the second pronunciation, which originated in the US, is gaining ground in British pronunciation, even if it is still regarded by many as being incorrect.

### controversy

CON-truh-vur-see or con-TROV-uhr-see? Again, the former is the older variant, with its adherents arguing that this stress pattern is closer to the Latin model from which the *contr-* element comes. However, usage is fairly evenly divided between the two, with the latter's stress on the second syllable becoming more popular, even though it is often frowned upon by purists.

## dispute

dis-PYOOT or DIS-pyoot? Many speakers use the former variant, with stress on the second syllable, for both the noun and verb forms. Some speakers stress the first syllable when the word is used as a noun, but the second when it is a verb. This pattern of usage applies more uniformly to words like *record*.

## cervical

SUR-vi-kuhl or suhr-VY-kuhl? In the UK and America the first pronunciation is widely used. However, as with *controversy*, there is a potential (although not especially strong) argument, based on the word's Latin origins, that the stress should fall on the second syllable. This is the pronunciation generally preferred in medical circles.

## research

The 'mispronunciation' of this word is the *bête noire* of some pronunciation-watchers. The traditional British form of the word, in both its noun and verb forms, has stress on the second syllable (ruh-SURCH). In America and elsewhere, an alternative form, REE-surch, is used for both noun and verb, and this form is becoming more widespread, especially for the pronunciation of the noun.

### Northern bits and bats

In 2004, the British Library posted on the Internet a sound archive of authentic northern English speech. It draws on thousands of hours of recordings, some going back to the 19th century when cylinder dictaphones were used. The north of England was chosen because of its particularly rich mix of accents and dialects.

Among the voices on the archive is that of a Lancashire sheep-farmer, Jim, who uses *happen* for 'perhaps', *aye* for 'yes', and *hae* for 'have', while a rabbit-catcher born in 1879 illustrates the Northumberland dialect in his use of *gan* for 'go', *mysell* for 'myself' and *hing* for 'hang'. A much more recent recording, made in 1999 with a Yorkshire-born prison inmate, demonstrates the resilience of words such as *bits and bats* for 'bits and bobs', *mam* for 'mum', and *carry-on* for a system or set-up.

# 16

# Speaking Englishes

I who have cursed the drunken officer of British rule, how choose between this
Africa and the English tongue I love?

Derek Walcott, *A Far Cry from Africa*, 1962.

English is the possession of every individual and every community that in any
way uses it, regardless of what any other individual or community may think or
feel about the matter.

Tom McArthur, *Oxford Companion to the English Language*, 1992.

When I arrived in Singapore, Eugene told me that I could survive by mastering
the all-purpose phrase, 'Is it?' (pronounced as 'Izzit?' in Singlish) which could be
used to express agreement or disbelief, or as an acknowledgement that I was
paying attention, just two handy words I could throw in whenever there was an
awkward gap in the conversation.

Hwee Hwee Tan, *Foreign Bodies*, 1997.

A study in the journal *Science* by David Graddol, an expert in the
development of languages, suggests that English is set to decline as a world
language, with Mandarin taking over as the new 'must-learn' language of
the future. Certainly within the next few years the number of people
speaking English as a second language may well exceed the number of
native speakers. Neither likelihood, however, denies the enormous global
influence of English today. One in five of the world's population speaks it
with some fluency. It is the official or semi-official language of over seventy
countries, and it plays a significant role in over twenty more.

As a result, English is indeed a world language, but not a monolithic one. Rather it is a 'family' which encompasses many different varieties, some of which are well established over several centuries (such as American English), and others which are much more recent, especially those localized Englishes that are rapidly developing in South-East Asia.

American English was the first strand of non-British English to become a dominant global linguistic force; its influence is enormous, driven by American TV, film, and music, and by the sheer power of the US as a nation. The following discussion focuses on varieties of English in other parts of the world, some well established, others quite new, especially those found in Asia and Australasia.

There are two types of language change in regions where other native languages sit alongside English. Some terms are straightforward, formed on existing vocabulary (such as the Indian **DisComs**, see below), whilst others are essentially absorbed from other languages. Words in this last category can often say something significant about the kind of influence the native cultures in question have—many of the Samoan terms entering New Zealand English, for example, are all about local customs and traditions.

## Indian English

English has long been a key spoken and written language of the Indian subcontinent, both in its own right and as mixed with Hindi, Urdu, and other languages. A common estimate is that there are around 50 million people in India who can speak English fluently, with a further 200 million who use different kinds of English on a regular basis. Tom McArthur, in his *Oxford Guide to World English*, sees English as the 'window on the world' and the 'primary link language' for the Indian subcontinent, a situation which is largely the outcome of the Raj and British presence in the region since the seventeenth century.

This widespread fluency in English, coupled with the availability of vast pools of cheap labour and relatively high educational levels, has led to many new employment opportunities for Indians in the information technology sectors and in the call centres of multinational companies, which are increasingly being based in India. Employees have to learn to speak a more 'British' or 'American' type of English, rather than the Indian

English they are accustomed to. One former call-centre worker, quoted in *The Guardian*, relates how 'employees transformed themselves to the point where they could successfully become British on the phone . . . people said "Cheers" to each other'.

If English is of importance in Indian daily life, there has been a recent and tangible move towards elevating the status of Hindi and other indigenous languages, particularly in national and geographical names. A leading Hindi politician, the leader of the Samajwadi Party, called in 2004 for a rejection of the colonial associations of the word 'India' and for the official name of the country to be changed to its Hindi name *Bharat* (from the *Bharata dynasty* in the Hindu epic the *Mahabharata*). He also promised that, if elected, the party would stop using English in official communications.

Despite such initiatives it is clear that English remains an integral part of Indian culture and society. Its function as a link between the various indigenous languages of the subcontinent is very likely to ensure that it continues to thrive and develop. The 2004 Indian elections have by themselves brought into prominence **FTVs** (first-time voters), **EVMs** (electronic voting machines), and **booth capturing** (the practice of forcing polling-station officials to acquiesce in voting irregularities). The following list includes further terms which have gained currency in recent times, and illustrates the dual mechanisms for new coinages—the adaptation of existing English vocabulary, and the adoption of terms from other native languages.

**DisComs:** abbreviation for 'distribution companies' (i.e. electricity distribution companies). The term has appeared since the privatization of power in certain Indian states and is probably modelled on **dot-com**, an online business venture.

**Pak:** short form for Pakistan and much used in the Indian press, with none of the offensive connotations of the word **Paki** in British English. The word often occurs in combination such as *Indo-Pak Cricket Series, Indo-Pak tour, Indo-Pak ties*.

**Generation Next** or **Gen Next:** an all-purpose term, used in reference to a second generation of products (such as motorbikes), as well as film stars, politicians, and, collectively, the young people of today. A recent headline in the *Times of India* proclaims: 'Gen Next rules Bollywood', leading a story about the sons and daughters of stars who have also taken up acting in Bollywood films as a career.

**yatra** (from Sanskrit, meaning 'a journey'): although the term originally meant a procession or pilgrimage, especially a religious one, it is now being used by Indian politicians to refer to the journeys they are undertaking to campaign in various parts of the country, especially when this spans several weeks and regions.

**uttapam** (from Tamil): a thick pancake made from rice flour, to which onions, tomatoes, chillies, etc. are added during cooking.

**rashtra** (from Hindi): nation.
Girls are made to repeat the songs and 'slokas' until they have learnt them by heart. Many poems are the staple of nursery school rhymes but with a twist in the end to reiterate the topic of Hindu rashtra.
   *Economic and Political Weekly*, April 2002, Sameekshe Trust, India.

**shadi** (from Hindi): a wedding. The term, which is well established, is being frequently used in the domain names of Indian dating agencies.
The wedding invitations are another matter entirely. Dholkis, mehndis, mayouns, milads, sham-e-rangs, ganas, shadi receptions, valimas—among the absurdly extravagant there is a card for each occasion.
   *Wasafiri* Autumn 2000 issue, University of London.

# South-East Asian English

The region of South-East Asia encompasses Malaysia, Indonesia, Singapore, Hong Kong, the Philippines, Cambodia, Thailand, Laos, and Vietnam. English has been present in the region since the seventeenth century; today, in the Philippines, local varieties are estimated to be spoken by around 40 million people. English is also predominant among Singapore's four official languages, and plays a crucial part in the life, education, and business activity of Hong Kong.

In 2003, Hong Kong was in the news for all the wrong reasons. The **SARS** (Severe Acute Respiratory Syndrome) outbreak began there in March of that year. At first, the disease was given other names in the Hong Kong media, such as 'atypical pneumonia' or 'mystery flu'. It was not until April that the World Health Organization's term 'Severe Acute Respiratory Syndrome' began to be used in Hong Kong's news reports. It was speculated that the delay in the use of the term was due to the unfortunate similarity between SARS and the abbreviation for Hong Kong's official title (HK SAR, for Special Administrative Region), and the consequent unwillingness of the HK authorities to use a term that seemed so closely linked to the region.

Meanwhile in China, television presenters were advised by the authorities in 2004 to stop mixing English into their broadcasts. Words used alongside Mandarin include **cool**, **darling**, and—again—**SARS**: all have been proving popular with urban audiences, while hybrid words are also emerging, such as **interwang** for the Internet. Some Chinese news presenters have even admitted to not knowing the Mandarin for **DVD** or for **CD**.

## Singlish

*Singlish*, or Singapore English, mixes English with common phrases in the Chinese dialects (mostly Hokkien, one of the principal dialects spoken outside China), and some Malay.

Common features include the use of the Chinese words **lah** and **ah** for emphasis (*don't be like that lah; I come tonight, ah?*), the use of the all-purpose conversational 'fillers' **is it** and **isn't it** (*you check out today is it?*), and the use of particles such as **off** and **on** as verbs (*off the light*).

Recent vocabulary includes:

**makan** (from Malay)**:** food, eating.
Of the 21,168 makan places in Singapore, 17,070 are hawker stalls. Take your pick!
  *www.makantime.com, 2004.*

**commuter:** light rail transport (*I go to work by commuter*). The LRT system in Kuala Lumpur is named **Komuter**.

**bo cheng hu** (from Hokkien, meaning 'no government')**:** used to describe a state of disorder where anything goes.
That place, really bo cheng hu, how to do business there?

**kiasu** (from Hokkien, meaning 'afraid to lose'): anxious not to miss an opportunity.
It is better to be a bit kiasu and over-react rather than under-react, because you never know what surprises await you, according to National Development Minister Mah Bow Tan.
*Straits Times*, 27 April 2004.

**rakyat** (from Malay): the people.
The orbit of real Malay society is this hinterland, the world of the rakyat, the citizens. This is both cultural truth and constructed colonial history.
Ziauddin Sardar, *The Consumption of Kuala Lumpur*, Reaktion Books, 2000.

## Australian English

Despite distinct divergences in pronunciation, the vocabularies of Australian and New Zealand English are broadly similar, as are the linguistic influences driving them. Both, however, are also heavily influenced by the breadth and diversity of their ethnic communities. In Australia, the absorption of terms from Aboriginal culture, particularly relating to flora and fauna, have helped to dilute the perception of their English as the stereotypical 'strine': it is now recognized as being more cosmopolitan.

The distinction between formal and informal vocabulary in Australian English is not as great as in other varieties of English. Rhyming slang, imported from London in the nineteenth century, is thriving (particularly as a means of euphemism, as in a **snakes** for 'piss', from 'snake's hiss': *I'm busting for a snakes*). Colloquialisms, too, are commonplace even in formal writing, and the addition of suffixes such as '-o' and '-ie' (**servoe**, for service station, **ambo** for ambulance officer, and **blowie** for blowfly) is one of the major mechanisms behind the formation of new words.

In 2004, the world's media gave particular coverage to the term **schoolies' week**, which occurs at the end of the final year of secondary school and a time when school-leavers visit places such as Queensland's Gold Coast for a week of wild partying.

Further words reflecting today's Australia include:

**toolie:** a young male who is not a school-leaver, and is older than school-leavers, but who attends schoolies' week in pursuit of sex, usually as a member of a group of similar males. The term derives from an informal sense of 'tool', meaning 'penis'.

**seachanger:** a person who makes a dramatic change in their lifestyle, especially by moving from the city to a seaside or country area. The term originated in the Australian TV programme *SeaChange*.

**barbecue stopper:** an issue of major public importance, which will excite the interest of voters. Prime Minister John Howard used the term in July 2002, when he asserted that the issue of balancing work and family commitments was a 'barbecue stopper'.

**double plugger:** a flip-flop sandal with an extra plug on either side where the thong attaches to the sole.

# New Zealand English

New Zealand English is a mixture of the varieties of English spoken by settlers from England, Wales, Scotland, and Ireland, and the Maori language of the indigenous population. The intensification of interest in Maori affairs over the last twenty or so years has meant a new familiarity with Maori words and concepts, with words such as **tino rangatiratanga** (sovereignty), **kawanatanga** (right to self-government), and **kaitiaki** (guardians) becoming more widely known. Non-Maoris have become accustomed to using the term **tangata whenua** (people of the land) for Maori, and the Maori name for New Zealand itself (**Aotearoa**) is gaining international currency.

Maori is responsible for some notable cultural and political references in New Zealand society. **Waka** (a canoe) becomes a political party, while **waka-jumping** is the leaving of one political party for another. New concepts have been introduced—temporary campsites in National Parks are called by the Maori term **nohoanga**, while **hui** has replaced 'meeting' for many bicultural functions, with reference made to **hui-hoppers** and **rent-a-hui** protestors. Another interesting addition is the noun **whangai** for someone who has been fostered or adopted, now also used as a verb (*I was whangai'd*).

In addition to a strong Maori influence, the increasing Polynesian population from the Pacific Islands is introducing Samoan words to New

Zealand: these include **pe'a** (the male waist-to-knee Samoan tattoo, reflecting the new trend for tattooing), **fa'afafine** ('transsexual'), and **aiga** ('extended family').

# African English

English is today the African continent's single most widely used language. Far from being uniform throughout, several different varieties have developed in the different regions of the continent.

Although South African English is the best known of the African varieties of English, other regional Englishes include those termed East African English (spoken in Kenya, Tanzania, Malawi, and Uganda) and West African English (spoken in countries such as Nigeria and Ghana). Each variety has its own characteristic vocabulary, which includes local borrowings and hybrid compounds, and grammar.

## South African English

The Republic of South Africa celebrated in 2004 ten years of democratic elections. The country has witnessed radical changes since the end of apartheid, with a new generation of black people gaining senior posts in multinational organizations and setting up their own successful businesses (in the townships the BMW car is otherwise known as a **Black Man's Wish**, showing as it does that a black person has really 'arrived'). In spite of such transformation it is still apparent that white people dominate the boardroom, and that black people are appointed to visible but powerless positions in so-called **cappuccino deals**. Meanwhile, other aspects of South Africa's new society are reflected in words such as those below.

**kwaito:** a style of popular music similar to hip hop, featuring vocals recited over an instrumental backing with strong bass lines. It is said to be the sound which defines South Africa's black youth, and was named after the 'Amakwaito', a group of 1950s gangsters in the Johannesburg suburb of Sophiatown. Linguistically the name derives from the Afrikaans *kwaai*, meaning 'angry, vicious'.

**scotchie** (also **scotch ring** or **scotch call**)**:** a 'missed call' which communicates some pre-arranged message or requires the receiver to call back at their expense, thereby saving the first caller the cost of the call.

**lekgotla:** a strategy planning meeting, especially one convened by government or the executive committee of an organization. The term is Sesotho for 'assembly', or 'council'.

**Tsotsitaal:** an Afrikaans-influenced township patois, which was originally a form of slang used by criminals (or *tsotsi*), typically spoken in the province of Gauteng. The name is a blend of *tsotsi* and the Afrikaans word *taal*, or 'language'.

**condomizing:** equipping young adults with condoms.
The condomizing message regarding sex made sexual behaviour overt . . . Adults have been making children sexually active—not preventing AIDS.
Professor Herman Conradie, *Fighting Crimes Against Children in South Africa*.

# West and East African English

**pombe** (from Swahili): beer.
You don't drink anything except cheap pombe or that poison you manufacture in your workshop.
A. Gurnah, *Paradise*, 1994.

**buka** (from Hausa): a small roadside stall selling food (especially in Nigeria).

**matatu:** (in East Africa) a minibus or similar vehicle used as a taxi. The term is Swahili, short for *mapeni matatu* meaning 'thirty cents', a flat fare charged in the early 1960s.
He pulled to the side of the road and sat with the motor running, watching a matatu, loaded past possibility with people and luggage and chickens and goats, lurch recklessly past her.
A. Shreve, *The Last Time They Met*, 2001.

**mzungu:** (in East Africa) a white person. The term is from Swahili *zungu*, meaning 'European'.
Mzungu, mzungu. That's all you hear walking down the street in Uganda. Yeah, sure, it's cute to have the little kids point at you and call excitedly 'Mzungu! Mzungu! . . . white man!
From a personal web log, 2002.

# Canadian English

Canadian English has its roots in the American English brought to Canada by loyalists in the American Revolution, with the addition of adoptions from indigenous languages and borrowings from French. Today, much of the English spoken in Canada is also found in the US, but terms (or new meanings of existing terms) that are specific to Canada are still emerging, and often reflect the differences in culture between the two nations. The latest edition of the *Canadian Oxford Dictionary* (2004) has redefined 'marriage' as 'the legal and religious union of two people' (previously 'of a man and a woman') to reflect the fact that same-sex marriage is now legal in Canada's three most populous provinces: British Columbia, Ontario, and Quebec. Other recent Canadianisms include:

**two-spirited:** first used among Native American peoples to mean homosexual, and now also adopted into official use to mean a 'gay or lesbian indigenous person'. The official acceptance of the term is evidenced by its use in the names of organizations or initiatives, such as the *Two-Spirited Youth Program*, administered under Vancouver's Urban Native Youth Association.

**allophone:** (especially in Quebec) an immigrant whose first language is neither French nor English. The term derives from Greek *allos* meaning 'other', and follows the model of *francophone*.

**spinny** (informal): mad, crazy.
**'Rhoda,' I said as I hung up. 'The spinny one,' Hank said.**
  S. Birdsell, *Chrome Suite*, 1992.

**suck:** a person who behaves obsequiously to someone in authority.

**hoser:** an uncultivated person; an idiot or fool. The term is often used to describe an unintelligent, inarticulate, beer-drinking lout.
**In the absence of any hard news, the wire service reports were left to focus on the casual thanksgiving weekend attire of National Hockey League commissioner Gary Bettman. We are told Bettman arrived in Boston on Friday wearing 'beige hiking boots, blue jeans, a flannel shirt and a ski jacket': A real hoser, eh?**
  *The Toronto Star*, November 1994.

# 17

# It's Earlier than You Think

In March 2000, a milestone in the history of the *Oxford English Dictionary* was reached with the launch of *OED Online* (*www.oed.com*). The collection of words with which the project launched provided the first glimpse of the results of the wholesale revision of the *OED* which started in the 1990s and is ongoing today—the first such revision to be carried out since the dictionary's original publication as the *New English Dictionary* between 1884 and 1928. The aim of the revision process behind *OED Online* is one of thorough re-examination—looking at every word that the vast dictionary contains in light of a century's worth of scholarship and the new resources it has generated.

The process of revising the *OED* has unearthed a myriad of interesting developments. The *OED* is, and always has been, a dictionary built on quotations. One of the main aims of the project from its outset was that this dictionary, unlike others, would illustrate the meaning and use of each word through examples of every stage in its history. To this end, the project mobilized an army of readers to search through literature recording examples of words as they were used in written texts. Today, with the growth of electronic corpora and online databases, editors working on the project have access to a vast wealth of information which could never have been dreamt of in the late nineteenth and early twentieth centuries. Earlier examples of use are discovered in this way, leading to what, in dictionary parlance, is called an 'antedating': for while there are words whose origin is positively known and datable, there are many more words whose exact date and place of origin will probably never be known. In the case of this majority of English words and meanings, the dictionary presents the first known instance of a word as it currently stands rather than the proven first use. As such there is always the exciting possibility of revealing an earlier example, and such finds are as much in the hands of the public as the editors of the dictionary themselves.

To date, the record-holder for an antedating is the entry for **mind**, the word for an Irish 'lunula', a crescent-shaped Bronze Age ornament worn as a necklace. This word was previously attested only in the mid-nineteenth century in a museum catalogue at London's South Kensington Museum. Thanks to the searchable electronic corpus of material collected by the *Dictionary of Old English* project in Toronto, however, this has now been spectacularly antedated from the nineteenth century to the Old English period, where it appears in a Northumbrian liturgical text.

Other striking antedatings generated by the revision process show us that more familiar objects have also been with us in our written records for longer than we previously thought. At the time of the first edition of the *OED*, the earliest example of the word **nightshirt** was in Thomas Hughes' *Tom Brown's Schooldays* of 1857. However, the *OED* revision process has unearthed an antedating of exactly two centuries in a letter by Sir Ralph Verney: 'If hee weare his night sheirts when hee goes into company, neither he nor they can be commended' (*Memoirs of the Verney family*, 1657).

Previously, the first recorded date for the term **madwoman** that had come to the OED editors' attention was the early seventeenth century, the word being found in Thomas Scott's *The Belgicke Pismire* of 1622. Thanks to the *Middle English Dictionary*, it is now known that such souls were already drawing attention to themselves as early as the Middle English period: '_an _e creatur thowt _at sche ran al abowte _e place, as it had ben a mad woman, crying & roryng' (*The Book of Margery Kempe*, latest 1438); 'So the quene was nyghe oute of her wytte . . . and waltred as a madde woman' (Malory, *Le Morte D'Arthur*, 1470).

Sometimes the earliest example of use found by the *OED* seems surprisingly late. For example, that for **newly-wed** as a noun was, until recently, less than 100 years old, and offered the following optimistic nugget of advice: 'A Newly-wed can live on Marmalade for about three months' (*Cosmopolitan*, 1918). With access to searchable online databases—in the case of this particular entry, the Chadwyck–Healey *Literature Online* database—*OED Online* has unearthed an antedating of more than three centuries (albeit one which doesn't reflect quite such optimism as the former): 'Suggesting feare shall make the newly wed, Be false, because she feares she is suspected' (Anthony Chute, *Beawtie Dishonoured*, 1593).

The following are some other substantial antedatings discovered during the revision process so far: **messy** (was 1843, now 1627), **memo** (was 1889, now 1705), **moaner** (was 1927, now 1628), **monologue** (was 1668, now circa 1550), **moussaka** (was 1941, now 1862), **ogreish** (was 1852, now 1729), **oldie** (was 1879, now 1799), **olive oil** (was 1774, now 1566).

While it is always interesting to find out that a particular word is earlier than one might expect, these antedatings can also have wider implications. Sometimes finding the earliest instance of a word means uncovering a sense of it which has so far been overlooked in the dictionary. In the Second Edition of the *OED* (published in 1989), the entry for **mobster** recorded the earliest use of the word from 1917. During revision, the following two eighteenth-century examples of the word were found: 'This might have been, had Stout Clare Market mobsters, With Cleavers armd attack'd St James' Lobsters' (*Catalogue of Prints and Drawings: Political & Personal Satires*, British Museum, 1735); 'Like Mobsters in a frosty Day, When they a Game at Foot-Ball play, And keep all honest Folks within Doors, Whilst they are breaking Shins and Windows' (Thomas Catesby Paget, *Dialogue in Hudibrasticks*, 1739).

Reading over these examples, it quickly becomes obvious that they are not referring to mobsters as we think of them today. In fact, these quotes represent an earlier, now obsolete, use of **mobster** in the general sense of 'a member of a mob or crowd', which had previously gone unrecorded within the *OED*.

## It isn't Shakespeare

Even small antedatings can amount cumulatively to a substantial rethink. Among the most prolific sources of the earliest known recordings of a word, or a new sense of an existing word, is Shakespeare, and rightly so. The revision of the *OED*, however, and particularly the searching of databases of historical material, has revealed earlier evidence of many of these words in the works of less well-known sixteenth-century authors. This can be seen in the following examples:

### neglected
Previously believed to have been first used by Shakespeare in *As You Like It* (1616), this can now be seen to have been around a generation earlier: 'When the treasure gatherd was, the sicke neglected laye' (Barnabe Googe, *Popish Kingdome* 23, 1570); 'Negletto, despised, neglected, forgon, contemned, lightly regarded, not set by' (John Florio, *Worlde of Wordes* 238/2, 1598).

### number,
in the sense 'metrical periods or feet; lines, verses'. First attributed to Shakespeare in *Love's Labours Lost* (1598), it has now been antedated in this sense to 1579: 'The numbers rise so ful, & the verse groweth so big, that it seemeth he hath forgot the meanenesse of shepheards state and stile' (Edmund Spenser, *The Shepheardes Calender*).

### nuncio,
in the sense of 'a messenger'.
Previously believed to have been first used by Shakespeare in *Twelfth Night* (1616), 'nuncio' is now antedated in this sense to the previous century: 'In the first Scene a Nuntio declareth the successe of Arthurs warres in France' (Thomas Hughes, *Misfortunes of Arthur*, 1587-8); 'The Nuntio Mercury gaue his Lute to the Pastor Apollo' (Abraham Fraunce, *Louely Coronis* in *Countesse of Pembrokes Yuychurch*, 1592).

### offenceless,
in the sense of 'inoffensive'.
Once first attributed to Shakespeare in *Othello* (1616 or earlier), this has now been antedated by the following: 'The murdring

▶

Knyfe for my offenceelesse crime, I see preparde to gore my
guyltlesse blood' (Thomas Howell, *Devises*, 1581).

Without in any way detracting from his contribution to English
literature—many of his poetic compounds still stand as first uses—
examples like these suggest that the image of Shakespeare as a
language innovator may prove to have been slightly over-estimated.

# 18

# Anything Goes?
## Changing Taboos

**Fuck-a-doodle-do!**
> Charles (played by Hugh Grant), in the film *Four Weddings and A Funeral*, 1994.

**Cecil Parkinson loathed me particularly because I used four-letter words in front of the PM, which he thought monstrously intimate.**
> Late MP and diarist Alan Clark, reported in *The Times* in 1999.

**Bringing new meaning to bang for your buck, the British company French Connection advertised its upcoming store here by announcing 'San Francisco's First fcuk,' in front of Union Square. Say 'dyslexically suggestive' three times fast.**
> *www.MisterSF.com*, 2001.

**The Royal Association for Deaf people . . . objected to an advertisement in *Playstation Plus* for *Kerrang!*, a rock music magazine. The advertisement showed four words spelt out in British Sign Language with a reference key at the bottom to translate the letters. The message was 'Turn it f*****g down'.**
> News item on the website of the Royal Association for Deaf People, 1999.

**The Filth and the Fury**
> Headline in the *Daily Mirror*, 1976, following a notorious interview with the Sex Pistols live on Thames TV.

**Pistol Fires A Last Shot**
> The *Sun*, 2004, on former Sex Pistols member John Lydon's departure from *I'm a Celebrity . . . Get Me Out of Here!*

In February 2004, in a now notorious episode in the British celebreality show *I'm a Celebrity . . . Get Me Out of Here!*, the former member of the punk band the *Sex Pistols* John Lydon accused the voting audience of being 'fucking cunts' for failing to vote him off the show. The broadcast was live. By the following afternoon, the network ITV had received fewer than 100 complaints from a total viewing audience of around 11 million. Twenty-eight years earlier, the same man, then 'Johnny Rotten', had appeared on Thames Television's live teatime show *Today* and used the word 'fuck' on several occasions. The repercussions were enormous. The presenter of the show, Bill Grundy, was suspended and the *Sex Pistols* were unofficially blacklisted from live appearances. Looking back even further, to 1965, the theatre critic Kenneth Tynan was the first to utter the 'f-word' live (as a reference rather than an expletive), doing so on the BBC during a late-night talk-show interview with Eamonn Andrews. The Corporation gave an immediate apology but could not stem the tide of outrage which flowed both in the House of Commons, where four separate motions were signed, and in a letter from the morality campaigner Mary Whitehouse to the Queen, in which she stated that Tynan 'ought to have his bottom smacked'.

What happened in the thirty years of television history in which each of these episodes occurred? Had the two words used by John Lydon become neutralized to the extent that viewers no longer cared? The question as to whether today's audiences are significantly more tolerant of words previously considered completely taboo is a fascinating one. The producers of *I'm a Celebrity* were less sanguine than its viewers, swiftly deciding on a 15-second delay between a live utterance and its transmission to give ITV's 'bleepers' a chance to act. They were not alone in introducing a means of censorship. In the US, and in the wake of Janet Jackson's now infamous 'wardrobe malfunction' during the half-time interval at the Super Bowl (in which she exposed her breast), the House of Representatives hastily passed in 2004 the Broadcasting Decency Enforcement Act. As a result, many US television broadcasters, like their British counterparts, introduced a delay in the transmission of live performances. On the radio, America's most notorious 'shock jock' Howard Stern was dropped from several stations for a perceived excessive use of expletives.

Within the British television industry there are official scales of obscenity which are matched to various watersheds in order to protect children. The use of the word 'fuck' before 9 p.m. is absolutely disallowed; 'cunt' cannot under any circumstances be spoken before 10 p.m. These times are for the most part strictly followed. Johnny Rotten's outburst on the *Today* programme in 1976 clearly went out before the watershed. His expletives on *I'm a Celebrity*, however, were aired after 10 p.m. To see the different levels of outrage incited by the two episodes as evidence of a decline in moral values may not be comparing like with like.

Other taboo words are each given their own watershed rating, including 'motherfucker', used by pop star Madonna just before the 9 p.m. watershed in a live broadcast of the 2002 Turner Prize ceremony for contemporary British art. The broadcasters of the show, Channel 4, received a reprimand, known as an 'intervention', from the television watchdog, the ITC—too many interventions of this kind result in a fine. When, on the other hand, during an episode of *The Osbournes* broadcast at 9.01, the word 'fuck' was used over thirty times, almost no complaints were received, in spite of the show being billed as 'family viewing'. This last example is an important one, as there appear to be a number of issues at play in the public's response to the use of 'taboo' language, one of which is context.

The situation in which strong language is used is one of the most decisive factors determining the level of public offence. If a TV show, or personality, is expected to be controversial, then the impact of an offensive utterance is significantly diluted. In a now-famous interview with Dustin Hoffman by the saucy chat-show host Graham Norton, the film star told his favourite joke involving the use of both the 'f' and the 'c' words. Few viewers would have been surprised or shocked by such language on Norton's show, but Channel 4 nonetheless received an intervention, suggesting a gap between public taste and the assumptions of a professional watchdog. Hoffman's joke was clearly told on impulse, whereas Johnny Rotten's outburst on the pre-watershed show *Today* had, as columnist Mark Lawson points out, 'the strong suspicion of premeditation. The Pistols wanted to shock.'

The specific charge made by a taboo word is just as important in determining public response. Most offensive words fall into a particular category, be it sex, racial type, or class. The stronger the link with its origin, 115 the greater the power to shock. It is those words which have lost much of their historical attachment, and which are neutralized over time, which are likely to lose their 'highly offensive' label. The first attested use of the verb 'fuck' recorded in the *Oxford English Dictionary* was in 1568, in the sense of 'to copulate', and it has retained its original meaning right up to the present day. Increasingly, however, it is being used as a general swear word in all sorts of grammatical categories—as an exclamation, a noun, a verb, in verbal phrases ('fuck up', 'fuck off') and as an adjective ('fucking'), with little or no reference made to sex (as chef Gordon Ramsay's prolific use of the word in the recent TV show *Hell's Kitchen* amply testified). There is also good contemporary evidence that 'fuck' is being used affectionately— indeed even 'cunt' (first use recorded in the *OED* as 1230 in the street name 'gropecuntlane') is heading in that direction, if more slowly. Terms such as 'silly old cunt' or 'daft fucker' are used today without, for some at least, striking any discordant note of abuse. In British films by writers such as Richard Curtis, including *Four Weddings and A Funeral* and *Love Actually*, the use of words such as 'fuck' lends characters an almost endearing quality, spoken as they are in a bumbling, often eccentric, and always utterly British way. Indeed such is the familiarity of many swear words that the British Board of Film Classification launched in 2004 a survey to determine whether their use is now acceptable in films seen by children.

Another word which has lost its sting is that of 'berk', defined as a 'stupid or foolish person'. Its origins, however, were certainly taboo, being slang for 'cunt', based on the rhyme with 'Berkeley Hunt', a beginning today's users of the term are largely unaware of. Meanwhile, the British tabloid *The Sun* printed the word 'punani'—beloved of the risqué comedian Ali G and meaning 'female genitals'—in full until it realized its literal meaning. The result on one occasion was an asterisked 'b****cks' sitting alongside the more offensive 'punani'.

If sexual explicitness is no longer decried, racial and religious insults are still highly charged, and the public response has kept pace with the dictates of the law. The codes protecting racial and religious groups from verbal abuse are strict, and the flouting of these codes in almost every context, even in comedy and caricature, rarely passes unnoticed. In 2004, 116 an advertisement for chocolate ice cream which used the first part of the nursery rhyme 'eeny meeny, miney, mo' (the second part runs 'catch a nigger by his toe') was denounced as racist and swiftly removed from British billboards. The policing of blasphemy can be particularly fierce, and it is not unusual for overuse of the exclamations 'Jesus!' and 'Christ!' to prompt more public complaints than the use of other words generally considered to be higher up in the taboo hierarchy.

There have been several recent instances of a particular group explicitly reclaiming a taboo word previously used against them. In these cases the potency of a taboo word depends entirely on the intent of its user. In one sequence of Eve Ensler's play *The Vagina Monologues*, women are invited to re-appropriate 'cunt' in order to empower both the word and themselves. 'Nigger', which originally, in the sixteenth century, was a neutral term, and which only began to acquire derogatory connotations in the middle of the eighteenth century, has today been reclaimed by black culture and become a common term in hip hop and rap (often spelt 'nigga'), while 'queer' is also used with pride and humour by the gay community. A further powerful example of this re-mapping of taboo territory came in 2004 with the attempt by businessman Abdul Rahim to reclaim the word 'paki' from racists. Rahim, who runs a small clothing business, gave one fashion line the label 'PAK1'. His decision provoked extreme and divided reactions. Chastised by some for inciting racial hatred, he also received support from those who shared his vision of returning the word 'paki' to its original meaning: 'Paki is just a shortened version of Pakistani,' Rahim maintained, 'its literal meaning is "the pure"— so why should anyone be afraid of being called "pure"?'.

As with all taboo language, some words can remain powerful weapons in the wrong hands, and we have some way to go before they are neutralized to the extent that they can be freely used by everyone. There is never a shortage of examples of resistance to strong language. The late MP Alan Clark once caused considerable offence when he referred in the House of Commons to Africa as 'bongo-bongo land'. US comedienne Sarah Silverman's use of the word 'chink' in a stand-up routine prompted a huge public outcry. Film-maker Quentin Tarantino discovered the difference between a taboo which is self-appointed and one which is used against others, when the frequent use of 'nigger' in his films came under fire: 'Quentin is infatuated with that word,' said film-maker Spike Lee, 'What does he want to be made—an honorary black man?' In 1999 an aide to the District of Columbia's mayor resigned after his use of the word 'niggardly' was deemed a racial slur (the roots of the two words are in fact entirely distinct). In 2004, the former football manager and commentator Ron Atkinson resigned after his reference to the Chelsea captain Marcel Desailly as a 'fucking lazy thick nigger' was unwittingly broadcast live to stations in the Middle East. In the same month, the owner of the British *Daily Express*, Richard Desmond, was also censured (albeit with fewer repercussions) for his behaviour at a meeting in which he goose-stepped around his boardroom and denounced all Germans as 'Nazis'. Shortly afterwards, his paper used the same term against the French National Party leader Jean-Marie Le Pen in its headline 'Stop Le Nazi'.

On television and radio, the health warnings given at the start of those programmes airing after the watershed are so frequent that their impact may be becoming devalued. Whether this is of any consequence to the viewers or listeners of such programmes is debatable. What seems to be more certain is that there will always be a category of language which is considered offensive, and which holds the power to shock whenever it breaks through the euphemisms we replace it with. The shock value will depend on the intent of the speaker and on the sensitivities of the listener. Which words will occupy that category is almost impossible to predict, but the assumption that we as a society are no longer shockable seems to be less likely than that our vulnerabilities have simply changed.

## The shock of the old

The breaking of taboos is far from new. Traditionally seen as the tenderest of Roman love poets, Catullus used language as abusive as any found in literature today in his attacks on political opponents. Of Caesar he wrote the Latin equivalent of 'Poof—you are a shameless wanker, a glutton and a gambler'.

Today, those words regarded as particularly obscene are generally terms for parts of the body and their functions, or for sexual acts. Typically Old English or Middle English, most of them were originally standard terms. Chaucer uses 'arse', and Shakespeare 'bum', while lavatorial words such as 'bollocks', 'cock', 'piss' (which even appears in the King James Bible), and 'shit' were all used freely. It was not until the seventeenth and eighteenth centuries that the terms fell into disfavour, and the Victorians were particularly influential in making certain words taboo.

'Fuck' and 'cunt'—probably the most obscene words in use today— have been considered taboo for centuries. It was not until the publication of D. H. Lawrence's *Lady Chatterley's Lover*, and the subsequent trial for obscenity in 1960, that the word 'fuck' began to appear in print.

Many oaths which are considered mild today were formerly considered highly offensive. 'Bloody' was printed as 'b—y' in Victorian times, being held to be blasphemous and to have its origins in the oaths 'God's blood!' or 'by our Lady'. In fact, it is a reference to 'bloods', a term used in the seventeenth century for young, upper-class men who drank excessively, and comes from the expression 'as drunk as a blood'. The use of 'bloody' by George Bernard Shaw in his 1916 play *Pygmalion* (in which Eliza exclaims 'Walk? Not bloody likely!') caused a sensation: as late as 1960 *The Times* was referring to it as 'the Pygmalion word'.

# 19

# Watching Tennis at Eastbourne:
## The Language of Euphemism

**Naughty bits restored to classics**
Headline in *The Guardian*, August 2000.

**Euphemisms are unpleasant truths wearing diplomatic cologne.**
Quentin Crisp, British actor and writer, in *Manners from Heaven*, 1984.

**A diplomat is a person who can tell you to go to hell in such a way that you actually look forward to the trip.**
Caskie Stinnett, American writer, in *Out of the Red*, 1960.

**It falls along the lines of a personal level of sharing that may not be appropriate for one of our employees to do while on the job.**
Spokesperson for American Airlines after one of their pilots asked passengers 'If you are Christian, raise your hand. If you're not, you're crazy.'

Euphemism, according to Henry Fowler in his celebrated *Modern English Usage*, is 'the use of a mild or vague or periphrastic expression as a substitute for blunt precision or disagreeable use'. Much of the power of euphemism lies in its flexibility: its applications can vary dramatically and embrace both benign and hostile intent, delivering disguise, irony, satire, kindness, or evasion according to the will of its user. Its subjects are equally diverse, and shift according to the social attitudes of the time. If the eighteenth century saw a strong need to tiptoe around gin or ale, the subjects for which we seek verbal camouflage today include drugs, ethnicity, and sex.

Modern business is another rich source of euphemistic expression. The last twenty years have seen the development of a whole new lexicon of 'management speak', including the euphemistic *downsizing, empowerment*, and *capability gaps*. Such 'weasel words'—words which cannot be taken at face value—almost always have a hidden agenda. A recent statement by an insurance company that 'some premiums will need to be revisited' would amply bear out the 'weasel' factor, as would the words of sales manager Tim in the successful TV series *The Office*: 'Team Leader doesn't mean anything . . . it's a title someone's given you to get you to do something they don't want to do for free.'

In some cases new euphemisms simply replace old ones which have themselves taken on all the negative connotations of the original. This process, termed by the linguist Steven Pinker the 'euphemism treadmill', can in extreme cases happen over and over to a single expression: the above example of *downsizing* is a euphemism for *making redundant*, itself a euphemism for *layoffs*, etc., as the following time-line shows:

**sack**, 1840s

   **lay off**, 1890s

      **give the air**, 1900s

         **make redundant**, 1920s

       **let go**, 1940s

         **deselect**, 1960s

           **downsize**, 1980s

              **halve the footprint**, 1990s

                **RIF** (as a verb, for 'reduction in force'), 2000s

Many topics which would never be openly discussed in previous centuries invite no such coyness today—translators of even the bawdiest of Greek and Roman texts by authors such as Catullus and Aristophanes are replacing the euphemisms of older translations with a directness of expression to rival any modern erotic novel.

Some subjects of euphemistic expression, on the other hand, have remained remarkably constant over time. Death, sex, and politics are all areas in which new terms constantly evolve, or in which old ones are revived. War also inevitably invites euphemistic description. Terms such as *constructive engagement* (as a prerequisite for *regime change*) were prominent in the West's defence of actions in Iraq in 2003, whilst during conflict *Blue on Blue* replaced *friendly fire* and *collateral damage* as the euphemism of choice for the accidental killing of allied forces by their own side. The distracting language of game playing was used to describe tactical manoeuvres, from *Pac-Man* (referring to the arcade game in which a large dot races around a maze eating up smaller dots), to *killboxing* and *mouseholing* (respectively, the construction of grid squares into which laser bombs are fired, and the blowing of an entry hole into the wall of a building). Even the act of killing received new forms of expression: the adjectives *degraded*, *deconflicted*, and *attrited* were all euphemisms coined during the Iraq conflict. Meanwhile, in the detention centre of Guantanamo Bay, the term *prisoner of war* was controversially replaced by that of *unlawful combatant*, a phrase seen by many commentators as a euphemism masking what was effectively a change in legal status.

Out of the battle zone, the words of war and its rationale became themselves the focus of attention. Contesting for the phrase of 2003 was *sexing up*, infamously used to describe the alleged *dodgy dossier* compiled by Tony Blair's government as a persuader to war, and understood by most as a euphemism for exaggeration, (and by others for downright lying, otherwise known, euphemistically, as the *avoidance of truth*). Downplaying, as opposed to exaggeration, was also evident in post-war rhetoric when evidence of *weapons of mass destruction* continued to prove elusive. President Bush noticeably shifted his criteria to encompass *weapons of mass destruction related programs* and the even more cumbersome *weapons of mass destruction program-related activities*.

Euphemism has served politicians for centuries. The UK government, since the inception of 'New Labour' in the 1990s, has been accused of founding its very principles in euphemism and spin. Those accused argue that euphemism is a useful and necessary tool for making highly complex ideas and policies comprehensible, justifying current phraseology such as *civil pioneers* and *new localism*. Others view it as a highly efficient but no less deplorable means of obfuscation. Certainly euphemism and its opposite ('dysphemism') can be employed in the same parliamentary exchange: whilst the British government speak of *indirect taxation*, the opposition clearly prefer the term *stealth tax*.

Euphemism can be used to dramatically different ends. As a tool for evasion, it has no equal. Tony Blair's use of the word *totality* ('I stand by the totality of what I said at the time'), when answering questions relating to the death of arms expert David Kelly, invited ridicule from Tories and newspaper columnists alike, and yet appeared to serve its purpose of deflection. In Iraq, the deaths of four American workers were described in a US military briefing as *an uptick in local engagements*. Conversely, some of the best examples of euphemism are those which are immediately understood by the initiated even while they try to evade, and the most colourful entertain in the process. 'I'm sorry if anyone was offended by the wardrobe malfunction during the halftime performance at the Super Bowl. It was not intentional and is regrettable,' read a statement from pop star Justin Timberlake, February 2004, after he popped off part of Janet Jackson's corset, exposing her breast.

Operating in the same way, the term *spin doctor* would be entirely opaque to any learner of English, and yet for native speakers much of its impact comes from its transparency. Similarly, we no longer question the meaning of a *full and frank discussion* in the political arena, nor that of a *robust exchange*: both indicate verbal fisticuffs between antagonists and a confrontation that is anything but polite. Here euphemism operates as a surprisingly direct code, in much the same way as slang and street-talk serve those in the know. When George W. Bush allegedly told former Labour communications director Alastair Campbell that 'your man has got cojones' (the Spanish for testicles), after Tony Blair had pledged British troops to the war effort, he assumed that his joke would be understood by his team alone: 'of course, these Brits don't know what cojones are'.

In celebrity gossip, too, euphemism provides a highly efficient shorthand, in this case with the important added function of evading legal consequences. Delivered to millions through celebrity magazines, newspapers, television and online chat rooms, details of the private lives of celebrities are wrapped in a whole new vocabulary of euphemistic innuendo, with playful or sinister intent. While such terms as *confirmed bachelor* and *long-term companion* may strike us today as unnecessarily coy and old-fashioned, recent speculation over the sexual preferences of high-profile personalities suggests a new creativity, reminiscent of a bygone era. 'I was always fond of *she watches the tennis at Eastbourne* and *he's frightfully musical, you know*', the broadcaster Simon Fanshawe is quoted as saying in a recent article in *The Guardian* newspaper. Such terms are the 'sort of phrases that emerged when the 50s were fading into the 60s and people suddenly had to find a way to talk about something they'd never talked about at all before'. If these colourful euphemisms disappeared long ago, they have been replaced by other, equally transparent allusions to the domestic lives of today's celebrities. Many are far from harmless and affectionate, and offer good examples of how euphemistic expression can be used to deliver biting insult. A companion to politician Peter Mandelson was described by one paper as his *dancing partner*, a phrase carrying the strongly implied criticism of a man who is 'not out' (*out* being another good example of a euphemism understood by all).

There will always be a need for euphemism. What is fascinating is how the subjects for which we need it are changing. If childbirth, mental illness, and bankruptcy demanded as much soft focus as language could give it in Victorian times, our squeamishness today has moved on to other subjects. There are bound to be some constants over the next hundred years—sex, money, and war will always need careful expression—but most telling will be the euphemisms we create for new subjects which require protection from the full linguistic glare.

## Euphemistic intoxication

**Gin,** 1700–1900
diddle
lightning
mother's ruin
satin
sweetstuff
strip-me-naked
tiger's milk
tittery
royal bob
needle and pin

**Cannabis,** 1900–
blonde
cheeba
ashes
bullyon
jive stick
jolly green
parsley
bazooka
gold

(from a UK government's advertisement in the wake of the downgraded classification of cannabis in 2004: 'Call it what you like, just don't call it legal'.)

# 20

# Figuratively Speaking

I love metaphor. It provides two loaves where there seems to be one. Sometimes it throws in a load of fish.
American writer Bernard Malamud, *Paris Review*, 1975.

And he leaps into the air like a big green lighthouse.
BBC commentator on Arsenal goalkeeper Pat Jennings, on *Match of the Day*, 1970s.

I wear the trousers. And I wash and iron them too.
Denis Thatcher, June 2003.

Brighton, a city that looks as if it is permanently helping police with their enquiries.
Columnist and commentator Keith Waterhouse, reported December 2003.

St Paul was the Alastair Campbell of Christianity: a born-again, on-message enforcer.
Writer A. A. Gill, July 2003.

Like a mackerel in the moonlight—it both shines and stinks at the same time.
Former Georgia senator and Vietnam veteran Max Cleland, attacking criticism from Ed Gillespie (the Republican National Committee chairman who did not serve in the military) of John Kerry's war record, 2004.

She was almost always surrounded by members of the sisterhood . . . This technique is known as a 'doughnut' and she managed to assemble a fine, frosted confection, a Krispy Kreme among parliamentary doughnuts.
Columnist Simon Hoggart, writing in *The Guardian* in 2004 about the Immigration Minister Beverley Hughes.

Figurative language is the language of images; it is the means by which words can invoke the senses and the imagination. Each of the devices of simile, metaphor, and idiom (of the non-literal kind) allows us to 'see' the substance of a speaker's or writer's words. They also enable us to instantly pick up the intention behind those words, be it humour, emotion, satire, or poetry.

We all use and experience non-literal language. Similes and metaphors may be associated in our minds with literature and grand words, but they are equally grounded in the language which surrounds us all the time. Adverts, newspapers, and television have long been rich sources of figurative speech at this everyday level. We may be unaware of the fact that we are using figurative speech, as for example in our unselfconscious use of the word 'literally' to introduce patently non-literal phrases, often with unintentional humorous effects: 'They bought the car and literally ran it into the ground'; 'We were literally killing ourselves laughing'.

## As easy as ABC: the simile

Each of us carries our own individual stock of similes, appropriated over time and inherited from parents and peers. We use them for humour, for adding vividness and colour, and, by appropriating (and creating) our own favourites, as an expression of individuality. No collection is static, and we take on board new ones as they suit. Equally, some older terms are thrown out: few teenagers of today would see the relevance of similes such as 'as sober as a judge' or 'as common as muck'. Others still are simply replaced: 'as cheap as dirt' is now more often 'as cheap as chips', thanks in part to the excitable exclamations of the British antiques-show presenter, David Dickinson. Other similes persist in spite of their having become untethered to the real world. Often used humorously and in silent homage to a past era, 'dead as a doornail', 'bald as a coot', and 'daft as a brush' are all still very much in evidence today.

As we grow more comfortable with discussion of sexual preferences, some of the latest similes to have appeared revolve around the gay/straight axis. So we see 'as gay as a window', 'as gay as a goose', or even 'as gay as a yellow duster', 'as queer as a coot/kipper', 'as camp as a row of tents', 'as bent as a nine-bob note', and 'as straight as a tie/shingle/loon's leg/die/yardarm/

broom handle/gun barrel'. Other contemporary favourites, with a more traditional feel, include 'sweet as a nut' and 'sound as a pound'.

Similes can also be deliberately ironic: 'as clear as mud', and 'about as exciting as watching paint dry' are both in widespread use, while others bear a more individual touch: a *New York Times* article once described the Republican Party's brand of conservatism as being 'as compassionate as a nail gun'.

We have television comedy to thank for some of the strangest similes: 'as thick as a whale omelette', and 'as cunning as a fox that has just been made professor of cunning at Oxford university' are just two of the many wildly inventive creations from the eighties' British series *Blackadder*. Other more recent surreal examples include:

**The dark is as black as a bogman's toejam, and the light is brighter than God's front teeth.**
Tom Robbins in *Fierce Invalids Home from Hot Climates*, 2001.

**My mouth was about as dry as a popcorn fart, and I had just about mustered up enough courage to speak.**
Robert J. Adams in *The South Road*, 2001.

**Their arguments are about as practical as jet-skis on the M1.**
*RCM & E*, 2003.

Others meanwhile are more straightforwardly entertaining:

**That's part of its tech appeal: a frenetic tinkerability that could keep you as busy as a nerd partitioning his hard drive.**
*Wired magazine*, 2000.

**They have assembled a scrupulously contrived and focus-grouped product that is as charmless as a verruca.**
*Daily Telegraph*, 2003.

**The change into second tends to become as notchy as a porn star's bedpost.**
*Max Power*, 2001.

# Mixing your metaphors

A mixed metaphor combines images or traditional sayings which, together, do not quite make sense. A mixed metaphor attempts to create an extended comparison but fails because it is not consistent with itself, and so it collapses. For one to have full impact, the images need to be both well known and incompatible. When the British Home Secretary David Blunkett announced that 'In the end the golden goose will be cooked', the mixed metaphor became a favourite topic of conversation. He was in good company. Ernest Bevin famously stated: 'Open that Pandora's box and who knows what Trojan horses will jump out?', while more recently the British Labour Party's former director of communications Alastair Campbell told journalists in the wake of the Hutton Report that 'we can dance on pinheads till the cows come home'. Following accusations regarding the subject of that report, namely the British cabinet's alleged 'dodgy dossier', a government spokesman announced that 'This is now a game of chicken with the Beeb. The only way they will shift is if they see the screw tightening'. George W. Bush is famous for mixing his metaphors, a linguistic attribute which is endlessly satirized; one spoof on a weblog of his inaugural address read: 'Surrounded as we are by terrorists, we must always have a mixed metaphor to rely on, and a ready sword to light the path to peace'.

Mixed metaphors are not the exclusive prerogative of politicians (although it clearly helps— Ann Richards, the Democrat governor of Texas, said of George Bush Senior: 'Poor George, he was born with a silver foot in his mouth'). Film mogul Sam Goldwyn once declared that 'that's the way with these directors, they're always biting the hand that lays the golden egg'. Newspaper headlines can be equally culpable: 'Assassin's knife clouds France's skies' ran one leader, while the respected New York Times columnist William Safire also over-enthused, announcing that 'editorialists began to hold their noses at echoes of the Smoot-Hawley trade barriers'. Meanwhile, an interview with the actor Rob Lowe caught him describing one of his fellow actors in NBC's *The West Wing* as someone who 'tees the ball up and hits it out of the park every time'.

# What's in an idiom?

Idioms, those phrases and expressions which add up to more than the sum of their literal parts, are among the most effective means of visualizing a concept through words. We use idioms all the time, both figuratively and non-figuratively. In the latter category, phrases such as 'got it in for', or 'labour the point', are examples of straightforward idiomatic language. It is the figurative idioms, however, which provide the greatest colour. While Shakespeare and the Bible remain two of the richest sources of modern figurative idiom, new coinages are constantly surfacing to meet the requirements of their time. As the world changes, so our stock of experiences changes too and demands new expression.

The following are figurative uses which have recently moved under the spotlight.

## Nailing jelly to a tree: idioms on the move

**flood the zone:** to send a large number of reporters and journalists to a major news event.
**Every move to address the fallout from the Blair scandal only invited more coverage. Raines, famous for flooding the zone on big news stories, ironically ended up drowning in the coverage.**
   *Time* magazine, June 2003.

**not boiling the ocean:** not trying to do anything superhuman. This business idiom expresses frustration at the inability to effect even the smallest changes.

**take the first thing smoking** (US): to take the first available flight or route out of somewhere. The idiom may have originated in the title of a book by Nelson Eubanks.
**Deciding she'd amassed enough of a fortune for the present, Champagne caught the first thing smoking to Chicago.**
   Blake Y. Moore, *Triple Take*, 2003.

**feel one's cheerios** (US): to feel strong and confident. 'He's feeling his Cheerios' was a slogan for the breakfast cereal from 1950–3, and is an extension of the phrase 'feeling one's oats'.
**A young Mafia buck, feeling his Cheerios, issued an insult, one that in this neighborhood with its ominous history, its sensitivities, its codes, inevitably drew a response.**

*New York* magazine, 2004.

**nailing jelly to the tree/the wall:** used with reference to solving a messy and intractable problem that is bound to fail. The term dates back almost a century but is coming back into play.

You can no more make an agreement with those leaders in Colombia than you can nail currant jelly to the wall. And the failure . . . is not due to the nail. It's due to the currant jelly.

Attributed to Theodore Roosevelt, 1903.

**harsh your mellow** (US): to upset you.

If you can't get the respect, man, then these people are just going to harsh your mellow and that's nothing but a bum trip to nowheresville.

Online discussion forum, 2004.

**feed the rat:** to get your adrenalin fix.

Even experienced climbers 'feed the rat' . . . on the Grand's Upper Exum Ridge Route.

*Outside* magazine, 2003.

**ice someone's grill:** to invade someone's personal space.

**a cockroach problem:** a problem which is bigger than it initially appears.

**mooning the giant:** to antagonize the leading player in a field, to 'awaken the enemy'. To 'moon' is to drop one's trousers as a gesture of rebellion or defiance.

There's a saying in techdom about Microsoft: Don't moon the giant. Crossgain mooned Microsoft every which way.

*www.businessweek.com*, 2001.

**call an audible:** to make people listen. One report from the front line in Iraq during the 2003 Gulf conflict stated that General Tommy Franks had *declared an audible at the line of scrimmage*, thereby also employing a powerful sports metaphor.

**shoot someone's fox:** to bring a contest to an unsporting end; to pre-empt something. Shooting foxes before a hunt is complete was traditionally seen as a disgrace. Despite current hostility towards fox-hunting, the phrase seems to be undergoing something of a revival.

I noticed at the time that there were no comments, cheers or shouts from the Opposition, because my right honourable Friend had shot most of their foxes in the lead-up to the budget.

Deputy Prime Minister John Prescott in the House of Commons, March 2004.

## Celebrity shorthand

The use of the names of public figures as a shorthand for a certain style or attribute is an area of transferred language which is notably on the increase. To be 'Bill Clintoned', for example, has meant various things over the past decade—its most recent sense describing someone affected by the charm of the former US President during his European book tour (and sporting what *The Guardian* reported as 'a dreamy smile and a deep cerise flush running down their neck'). Celebrities meanwhile can become certifiable brands in themselves: 'I went to see the new Jim Carrey last week' is explanation enough, without the need for a film title, while across America, 'doing a Jessica' has become a synonym for ditziness thanks to Jessica Simpson and her TV reality show *The Newlyweds*. Allusions to fictional figures are also strong workers in figurative speech. David Beckham's haircuts took on added resonance for the newspapers following successive and lurid allegations of adulterous affairs: 'Gone was the Legolas look, banished the ponytail. In its place, a no-hair haircut redolent of Buddhist humility' wrote *The Times* in an article which began 'I have measured out my life in photo opportunities' (thus modifying the nicely figurative words of T. S. Eliot's Alfred Prufrock: 'I have measured out my life in coffee spoons').

Idioms, metaphors, and similes will always be part of language's strongest armoury. Their strength as devices lies in their ability to adapt to their times and to keep pace with modern conversations, observations, and trends. Above all, the images they draw on must be relevant. Whether 'harshing your mellow' and 'cheap as chips' stay around, or are quickly superseded, they are clearly telling us something about now.

# 21

# The Language of Events

**The world is but a word.**
William Shakespeare, *Timon of Athens*, 1604.

Language, as the American lexicographer Anne Soukhanov neatly put it, 'is an uncompromising mirror ... an unretouched record of the thoughts, feelings, dreams, successes, failures, and intent of the people'. We are what we say, and the ways in which events and words connect are multifold. Language can be the instigator of change, it can direct events once they have started on their course, and it can sum up an event in just a few words so that those words and the incident itself become inextricable.

## Sexing up and getting up

The most dramatic encounters between historic events and language occur when words become direct agents as well as descriptors, instigating major change. In Britain, what became known as the David Kelly affair brought the choice of politicians' words directly under the microscope. Those chosen by British journalist Andrew Gilligan in a broadcast report in May 2003, in which he accused the British government of both exaggeration and distortion of the threat posed by Saddam Hussein, were judged by the subsequent Hutton Inquiry to be the catalyst for a whole series of events, including the death of arms expert David Kelly. The events which followed were to dominate political debate and public scrutiny for many months.

Two terms in particular preoccupied the headline writers. The first, **sexing up**, was a powerful two-word distillation of the accusation by Gilligan that the government had embellished its dossier on Iraq with intelligence known to be false or unreliable. The subsequent Hutton report into the accusation concluded that Gilligan's use of language was careless and his words unfounded, a verdict shared later by the BBC which went into turmoil in the wake of the report's criticisms and which was subsequently castigated by its staff for its own language, this time one of apology and humility. Meanwhile, the verb 'sex up' acquired a life of its own, and began to be applied to a whole variety of contexts, from celebrity makeovers to science. 'Viagra to sex up Super Bowl', ran one headline in India's *Economic Times*, describing the ad breaks planned during the screening of the major American football event.

The second term, the tag of **dodgy dossier** given to a government briefing document about Iraq and its capabilities, was first used in a leader published in Britain's *Observer* newspaper on 9 February 2003. Few people that Sunday could have guessed how rapidly the term would become shorthand for the Blair government's alleged spin-doctoring in its rationale for war. It too looks to be moving outwards, if not as dramatically as 'sexing up'. 'Dodgy dossier syndrome rife in the workplace', and even 'Louis XIV's dodgy dossier' (an account of the seventeenth-century scandal, 'The Affair of the Poisons'), are some recent examples of the term appearing in unrelated contexts.

The **45 minutes** claim at the heart of Gilligan's story, namely the deliberate implication made by the British government that Iraq could launch weapons of mass destruction within that short a time, also began to appear in surprising and often amusing contexts. When, in a match in February 2004, the British football club Manchester City went from 0–3 down to beat Tottenham Hotspur 4–3, it was almost inevitable that the second half of the match was headlined **45 minutes of mass destruction**.

Against this backdrop, the language of almost everyone involved in the run-up to war in Iraq came under scrutiny. Alastair Campbell, then the Director of Communications for the Labour Party and as such intricately involved in the affair, was even said to have created his own private lexicon in his personal diary accounts. In an entry about the defence secretary Geoff Hoon, he claimed that the government wanted to '**get up** [the] source'. This phrasal use of the verb 'get' may yet require the addition of a new definition in future dictionaries, namely the release of a source's

identity into the public domain, perhaps in the sense of 'getting them up' above the parapet. Comment was also made on the fact that Campbell alone used the word **truth** in his response to the findings of the Hutton enquiry ('The Prime Minister told the truth, the Government told the truth. I told the truth. The BBC did not tell the truth'), while the response of Tony Blair combined a restrained triumphalism with the less expected vocabulary of therapy, speaking of **drawing a line**, **moving on**, and **closure**.

## The emperor's new clothes

**I am not from these parts . . . I am from a little place called England. We used to run the world before you.**

British comedy actor Ricky Gervais, on accepting a Golden Globe award in Hollywood in 2004.

When Clare Short, the British secretary for international development, made her much-threatened exit from Tony Blair's cabinet in protest at the alleged bugging of UN staff in the build-up to war in Iraq, she launched a new broadside at her ex-boss by referring to him as an **emperor**. The subsequent play on words by bloggers in their virtual diaries was fascinating, with **emperor's new clothes** becoming the phrase of the moment. George W. Bush, Tony Blair, and even Lord Hutton were implicated. Under the headline 'Suits you Sir: but can we suggest something warmer?', writer Terry Jones created an entire sketch in the *Independent* newspaper, retelling Hans Christian Andersen's story of the naked emperor who persuaded the populace that he was wearing the finest clothes. 'Reaction to Lord Hutton's report', wrote Jones, 'has been divided. The Emperor's staff are said to be ecstatic, and the Emperor himself has stated that "the lie that I was walking around without any clothes on has now been proved to be the real lie".' The impact of the message that we are entering a new age of deception, where no one can trust their own eyes and minds, was a powerful one. Columnist Matthew Parris continued the theme by pronouncing what he saw as Blair's pathological optimism to be further evidence of 'The Madness of King Tony'.

## Smoking pistols

When deliberation over language follows a major event, it can determine that event's subsequent direction. Such influence was demonstrated powerfully during the impeachment trial of Bill Clinton, and most famously in his statement, 'It depends on what the meaning of 'is' is', argued by many to signal the collapse of presidential integrity. The language of the prosecution in that trial of 1999 carried itself strong echoes of the Watergate affair twenty-five years before, and in particular of the articles of impeachment drafted against Richard Nixon. Accusations against Clinton of an **abuse of power**, and of the **repeated and unlawful** invocation of privilege to aid concealment, were seen as a deliberate linguistic exercise to imply misdemeanours of the same magnitude as those committed by Nixon, against whom the very same words were used. Even headline writers found useful resonance in the past, when Nixon's **smoking pistol** was metamorphosed into Clinton's **smoking bimbo**, an oblique reference to the cigar with which the President was said to have performed sexual acts on Monica Lewinsky and a phrase which took its place among other punning descriptions such as that of Clinton's **nuts and sluts defense**. **Smoking guns** were in the news again in 2003, when Hans Blix, the UN's chief weapons inspector, insisted that his team had failed to find any.

## Bottling history

If history could be bottled, the words used to describe it as it unfolds would preserve it almost perfectly. Language can provide such an immediate summary of an event that a single word or phrase can become its shorthand. The original context of the term is never quite lost, so that all subsequent uses, even those which play on its words, are underpinned by that first reference point. **The night of the long knives** has remained a sinister distillation of Hitler's purging of his own ranks, and all metaphorical uses of the phrase today carry its history with it. The term was turned to comic effect during the British Lib-Lab pact of 1978, described by a wag as **the night of the long spoons**, a statement which again relied on a knowledge of the original. Margaret Thatcher's celebrated and defiant response to pleas for a U-turn—**This lady's not for turning**— also owed much of its resonance to its source, the title of Christopher Fry's 1948 play about a woman's resistance to a witchcraft trial, *The Lady's Not for Burning*. Twenty-three years later, Tony Blair suggested unexpected parallels with a former Prime Minister facing disquiet in their ranks, in a speech to his own party which included the words: **Forward or back. I can only go one way. I've not got a reverse gear**. This last statement was gleefully returned to by the Conservative opposition when Blair did, indeed, make a U-turn in his decision to put membership of the European Union to a referendum.

It would be hard today to mention the term **ground zero** without evoking an immediate memory of **9/11**, or 11 September 2001, itself now a reference embracing a whole series of emotions and political actions which stretch far beyond that single date. More recently still, the two-word term **road map** now appears to be freely used in political contexts and to be quickly understood as a contraction of **road map to peace**, a plan designed by the US to bring accord to the Middle East.

Although language never stands still, it does not erase its history as it goes. Some of the most powerful and colourful events of the past are preserved through words which will forever be linked to the history they describe, even as they are taken up by others to fit newer realities.

## Queen of people's hearts

The airing in March 2004, by the US television network NBC, of the 'secret tapes' of Diana, Princess of Wales, in which she tells biographer Andrew Morton of her ill-fated marriage, brings inevitably to mind one of the most notable interviews of the twentieth century, one conducted by journalist Martin Bashir with Diana in November 1995. Over 22 million people watched the interview, which appeared on British television's *Panorama* programme, and its impact on the public perception of the royal family was enormous. Until that moment Diana's native language had always been the image, rather than the word. It was in pictures that she was best known, and this occasion was one of the very few when she was heard to speak freely.

Whilst Diana had not arranged to see the questions that she was to be asked, it is believed that she was acutely aware of the ground that the interview would cover. Her language throughout, engaging and apparently spontaneous, nonetheless betrayed at times a careful preparation, particularly in her use of certain carefully crafted phrases. **There is no better way to dismantle a personality than to isolate it**, for example, sounded more like a self-help mantra than words which would have come naturally

▶

to Diana herself. Her celebrated statement that **there were three of us in the marriage, so it was a bit crowded**, sounded equally rehearsed, if no less effective for it. Most memorably of all, perhaps, her expression of the defining desire of her life, namely to be **a queen of people's hearts**, found a resonance which inspired many comments about her throughout her subsequent life, ending with Tony Blair's tribute on her death when he declared her to have been **the People's Princess**.

# Word Histories

> **The roots of language are irrational and of a magical nature.**
> Jorge Luis Borges, Argentinian poet and author, in *El otro, el mismo*, 1964.

> **Stability in language is synonymous with rigor mortis.**
> Ernest Weekley, British philologist, in *The English Language*, 1929.

> **The workings of language are as far from our awareness as the rationale for egg-laying is from the fly's.**
> Canadian linguist Steven Pinker in *The Language Instinct*, 1994.

The *Oxford English Dictionary*, making as it does a chronological study of words and their evolution, is a captivating record of language change. It offers thousands of word histories together with clues, through quotations from each period of a word's 'life', of how society moulded them. The routes that words take can often appear quite random—sometimes even perverse—and yet a closer look can highlight the extent to which vocabulary is a servant to our continuously changing needs. It seems a big leap for a word such as **animosity** to evolve into its meaning today, when in the fifteenth century it denoted spiritedness and courage, or for **emotion** to mutate from a public disturbance into the mental feeling it describes today. The development of such senses, however, is more often than not entirely logical. Today, 'animosity' retains its sense of spirit, albeit now one of enmity, whilst 'emotion' still describes a disturbance or agitation, only one now more limited in its application to the mind. More dramatically perhaps, **silly** has moved from its original meaning of 'deserving compassion' to 'foolish', whilst conversely **nice** started off as 'foolish' and has ended up as 'pleasant', embracing 'wanton' along the way.

The stories behind such changes are sometimes lost, but they are seldom without rationale.

The development of new meanings is an important mechanism in word coining. Around fifteen per cent of all new words are old words reinvented, a level which has remained remarkably constant throughout the history of English. **Wicked** is one of the most prominent examples from recent times, used as part of the teen lexicon with no trace of the nastiness with which it has been associated for over seven hundred years, and now used as a positive term of approval equivalent to 'excellent'. While less easily explained through etymology, the transformation of the word in its new context is a good illustration of the intentions behind slang, as a code to be understood by a select few, and a badge with which to signal 'belonging'. The result is often language used subversively: the turning of words on their head to signal difference or for purposes of disguise. **Bad** too became, as early as 1928, a word of high approval among the young; its influence, as with much of today's slang, was the vernacular of jazz and Black English, originating in the US. Many of today's hippest adjectives follow the same path: **hectic**, **rough**, **savage**, **radical**, and **heavy** are all now used to indicate approval.

## Changing direction . . .

The taking on of a new meaning is not the only way in which a word can change its direction. Some words change their part of speech, so that a noun, for example, becomes a verb, or a verb a noun. One of the most prolific examples today is the word **text**, which in the age of the mobile phone has metamorphosed from a noun into one of the most frequently used new verbs around today. Other words which have flipped over into a new category include to **blade** (to rollerblade), to **black-hole** (to cause something to disappear), to **bag** (to fit a patient with an oxygen mask or other respiratory aid), to **gift** (to give a present or donation to someone) to **message** (to send someone a message, particularly a text or email), to **guilt** (to make someone feel guilty), to **celeb** (to use one's celebrity to promote a cause, also known as **cause-celeb**), to **wife** (to downplay a woman's professional achievements in favour of her abilities as a mother or housewife), to **office** (to perform mundane office tasks such as filing or photocopying), and to **version** (to create a new version of something). Verbs which have moved over into nouns include a **spend** (the amount spent), and an **ask** (a desire or expectation, used particularly in football speak of **a big ask** and in the business term **best ask**, meaning the lowest quoted price).

The following are all examples of words which, while retaining their traditional meanings, have also acquired entirely new senses. Beneath each item is an indication of some of the more interesting aspects of its history, using the *Oxford English Dictionary* as a source. Some will survive in their new guises, while others will revert to type. Most fascinating of all, others still will move on in step with their new environments, and take on senses we cannot hope to predict.

**fascia:** a covering for the face of a mobile phone.
The original meaning of the term, dating back to the 1500s, describes a long, flat surface of wood, stone, or marble, especially as used in an architrave.

**zipper:** a display of news or advertisements which scrolls across an illuminated screen mounted on a building.
'Zipper' was first registered as a trademark in 1925, albeit in the sense of 'boots made of rubber and fabric'. At the same time, the term began to denote the fastening to which we still refer today. The latest sense development, as described above, picks up on the idea of things moving quickly in a straight line.

**sticky:** attracting long or repeated visits from users as a measure of a website's success.
The more common meaning of the adjective, of having adhesive qualities, began in the eighteenth century.

**fierce:** (Irish) very, extremely.

Chaucer was one of the first recorded users of the adjective 'fierce', using it to denote someone of formidably violent temper. The term also came to mean 'ardent', or 'eager', both of which form a bridge between the first meaning and the latest adverbial sense in Irish vocabulary.

**chemical:** an addictive drug.

The term was first used in reference to alchemy in the sixteenth century.

**lush:** sexually attractive.

In the fifteenth century lush meant 'soft' or 'tender'. The literary currency of the sense of 'verdant' and 'luxuriant' was probably due to Shakespeare's *Tempest*: 'How lush and lusty the grasse looks'.

## Chav

Not all word histories depend on a long lineage of previous meanings. The origins of very recent coinages, which have so far enjoyed only the briefest of lives, are often compelling—they represent language change in action. Other words, meanwhile, may have flown under the radar for many hundreds of years before bursting into wider popular use. The origins of words in this latter category are often among the most fascinating, given the long gap between their creation and their popularity. Such a word is **chav**, a term which is rapidly gaining currency, and which is a contender for the word of 2004.

The phenomenon of 'chav' was probably started by the website *chavscum.co.uk*, a site which presents itself as 'a humorous guide to Britain's burgeoning peasant underclass'. It was taken up by users of the influential *www.popbitch.com*, an irreverent celebrity-gossip bulletin board, populated chiefly by people working in the media and entertainment industry. Large articles appeared in quick succession in several daily papers, demonstrating the way in which websites can popularize new words. 'Chav' encapsulates the rise of what Jemima Lewis, writing in the *Sunday Telegraph*, described as 'the non-respectable working classes: the dole-scroungers, petty criminals, football hooligans and teenage pram-pushers'. Others have defined it by means of another popular term of class-related insult: 'council'. The *chavscum* website issues a guide to spotting such subjects, including their supposed dress code of baseball caps, trainers, branded shirts and jackets, and, in particular, thick gold chains and rings collectively termed **bling-bling**.

If the intention behind the creation of 'chav' was light-hearted, the label has caused alarm in liberal circles who see it as a resurgence of class prejudice. Descriptions of the phenomenon, however, continue unabated, with the result that the word 'chav' is becoming further entrenched in the language. As it does so, new derivatives seem to appear almost daily, offering a colourful illustration of language change. **Chavspotting** has, apparently, become a national pastime, and **celebrity chavs** (as opposed to ordinary **chavsters**) are a major focus area. Most recently, the adjective **chavtastic** has emerged and looks set to take its place in the 'chav' lexicon.

The precise origin of 'chav' is a matter of debate, but most people agree on its geography, namely that it probably began in Chatham, Kent, where it was best known until it gained its recent high profile. It seems that the word itself began as a derogatory label for an older underclass, gypsies, many of whom have lived in that area for generations. Language expert Michael Quinion surmises that 'chav' may well come from the Romany word for a child, *chavi*, recorded from the middle of the nineteenth century. Later in the same century it was apparently used as an insult to an adult man, after which it fell into obscurity before its revival today.

English will always change in accordance with our demands and fashions: as they change, so our language will modify to meet them. Its route can sometimes take dramatic turns, as in the case of **luxury**, which started its life with the meaning of 'lust' or 'lechery'. At other times the changes will be so subtle that we are completely unaware of anything happening at all. Word histories have no ending: no part of language can be guaranteed to stand still. Because of this, there will be many future episodes in each word's individual chronology, each of them begging the questions 'Why?' and 'How?'. To find the answers is to better understand the patterns in our history.

# 23

# Reading TV

Sharon: Aw, Kimmy, I think it's nice your mum's got a boyfriend. Or are they de factos?

Kim: De facto, night facto, the fact that they're facto-ing at all I find repulsive in the extreme.

> Quote from an episode of *Kath and Kim*, 2002.

No, no, no. This isn't out of the blue. This is smack dab in the middle of the blue.

> Chandler to Eddie after asking him to move out, in a 1994 episode of *Friends*.

I'm a Deity. Get me into there.

> Rod Liddle, writing in *The Times*, on a BBC show in which viewers were invited to vote on the modern relevance of God.

We're so over we need a new word for over.

> Carrie, speaking to Big, in an episode of *Sex and the City*.

I could catch a monkey. If I was starving I could. I'd make poison darts out of the poison of the deadly frogs . . . Prick yourself and you'd be dead within a day. Or longer. Different frogs, different times.

> *The Office*'s Gareth on how he might survive in the jungle.

It wasn't that long ago when correspondents on . . . MSNBC were enthusing about President Bush's aircraft-carrier landing as 'the president's excellent adventure'.

> *New York Times*, November 2003.

In 2004, a British comedy dating back to the 1980s was announced as the winner of 'Britain's Best Sitcom' poll, run by the BBC. The victory of *Only Fools and Horses* over more recent TV output was enough in the eyes of some critics to overthrow the notion that we are enjoying a golden age of British comedy. Less controversially perhaps, the result also highlighted one of the key components in successful television, and particularly comedy: a clever use of language which catches attention and which lingers in the public mind. It is not coincidental to the poll's outcome that many of the catchphrases of *Only Fools and Horses* ('luvvly jubbly', 'you plonker') are still current, nor that many of them are now absorbed into general vocabulary. Successful television, it would seem, allows its language to be shared as well as enjoyed.

More recently, one of the most linguistically creative shows has been the Australian sitcom *Kath and Kim* (shown in the UK on the channel LivingTV). The humour of the show, presented without a canned-laughter backdrop, is both black and cruel. Both of the main characters—the mother and daughter in the show's title—speak in comically exaggerated Australian vowels, rooted in the fictional Melbourne suburb of Fountain Lakes which they inhabit. Its geographical roots, announced every time Kath pronounces 'that's noo . . . iice' and 'look at moy', are crucial to its success. 'My marriage is over. O.V.A.H. Over', Kim tells her mother. Wordplay, mixed metaphors, and malapropisms are at the heart of much of the show's comedy (as in the title itself, which plays on the term 'kith and kin'). 'I want to be effluent, Mum', Kim announces, while her mother declares that her daughter is burning the candle 'at both ends of the spectrum'. Words are deliberately misunderstood, underscoring the absurdity of the situations the characters find themselves in. Kath, confused about her daughter's sexuality, suggests that Kim is 'a Dutch seawall'—in other words, 'a dyke'. Another time she tells Kim that 'you may eat like a pig but you're certainly not a dog', to which her daughter replies 'so how come I have a bitch for a mother?'. Such clever dialogue, in which language is explicitly deliberated over, is not incidental to the growing cult status of *Kath and Kim* in and outside its Australian homeland.

As the cult of *Kath and Kim* was just beginning, that of three American series came to an end—in viewing terms at least. The last episodes of *Sex and the City*, *Friends*, and *Frasier* were all broadcast in the course of 2004, marking a conclusion to long-running shows which have been among the most trendsetting and iconic in many decades. Their linguistic legacy may yet live on. Sali Tagliamonte, a linguistics professor at the University of Toronto, suggests in a new study of over eight years of 'Friendspeak' that the series has been in the vanguard of changes in the way Americans talk. The ways in which Joey, Chandler, Ross, Monica, Phoebe, and Rachel speak, inflect, and wordplay are now undoubtedly the features of a generation. After tabulating over 9,000 adjectives used in the show, Tagliamonte concludes that its greatest linguistic influence has been the intensifier 'so' ('that is so yesterday'), replacing 'really' in the teenage and twenty-something lexicon. *Friends* offered the perfect showcase for the way in which language was already evolving, helping to open up new but geographically or socially limited patterns to a vast and receptive audience. If not the creator of the intensifying 'so' and 'totally', it certainly contributed to its success, pushing the envelope of something already defined.

The first role of catchphrases is to act as linguistic signatures for a character, and ultimately for a show itself. Some are so powerful that they quickly become lodged as part of everyday speech, ultimately losing their original reference point. 'Bada bing', born in the classic film of the 1970s, *The Godfather*, was dramatically revived by the US mafia drama series *The Sopranos* and has since taken off. Its applications can be wildly varied—it has become the name of choice for new strip clubs, following the example of the show itself—but it is also colourfully used to emphasize the effortless consequences of an action ('I told him I'd call the cops, and bada bing, he gave it back'). In one of its most recent incarnations, used on its own or in the phrase 'bada boom bada bing', it serves as a modern alternative to 'QED'—a form of 'there you have it'. Finally (although probably not in the lifetime of the phrase), evidence is emerging of 'bada bing' meaning genitalia: 'getting out their bada bing!'

A phrase from another highly successful series, *Seinfeld*, namely 'Yada yada yada', has also claimed linguistic independence as an alternative to 'blah blah blah' ('I gotta tell you,' says George in an episode of the series titled

'The Yada Yada', 'I am loving this yada yada thing. I can gloss over my whole life story.') Equally, 'voted off the island', from the reality survival show *Survivor*, in which the public decides who has to leave, has branched out to the extent that figurative uses abound.

The differences between British and American television can be striking. While many of the most successful shows to come out of the US—such as *The West Wing* and *Sex and the City*—portray a slick, glamorous world, those of the UK seem to delight in characters who engage through their ineptness and dysfunction. It is through language that these differences are often distilled. David Brent, the hapless and manically voluble manager of *The Office*, is a modern-day (if more spiteful) successor to Basil Fawlty of the 1970s comedy *Fawlty Towers*: both would collapse if their self-delusion failed, and both unwittingly rely upon platitudes which they hold up for approval. Much of the humour of *The Office* comes from the use of clichés and management speak to parodic effect. 'Life is just a series of peaks and troughs', announces Brent, 'and you don't know whether you're in a trough until you're climbing out, or on a peak until you're coming down. And that's it you know, you never know what's round the corner. But it's all good. "If you want the rainbow, you've gotta put up with the rain."'

The world of David Brent's and Basil Fawlty's imagination is a surreal one; comedy ensues when they find themselves tripping over reality, which they do again and again. The setting of *Little Britain*, one of the best-loved British sketch comedies since *The Fast Show*, is equally strange: a twilight world of misfits who belong nowhere if not in an alternative Britain. Recurring characters are perfectly summarized by their language: the schoolgirl rebel Vicki Pollard's frequent mumbles about 'this fing wot you know nuffin about', and her catchphrase 'yeah but no but yeah but', both powerfully mock habitual teenspeak. In *Cutting It*, one of Britain's best-loved contemporary dramas set in a hairdressing salon, a specially created Manchester slang sits alongside traditional colloquialisms and neatly reflects the programme's fusion of the everyday and the surreal. So notable is the series' use of language that the *Sunday Times* featured a short lexicon of the new Mancunian vernacular, including 'biscuit' (hard cash). 'gravy' (money, or sexual interest: 'what do you care where Gavin tips his gravy?'), and 'bleek' (to express shock or surprise, as in 'what the bleek?!'). Once again, the show's quotability goes a long way in accounting for its success.

◎

The language of such quintessentially British comedy is a long way from the urbane observations of President Jed Bartlet in *The West Wing*, or from some of the word-perfect exchanges of *Sex and the City*. 'Money is power, sex is power, therefore, getting money for sex is simply an exchange of power', pronounces Samantha in an episode from the latter, to which Carrie expertly replies: 'Once again, Samantha managed to up-sex me'. In another, Miranda poses the rhetorical question, 'Whatever happened to growing old gracefully?' 'It got old,' Carrie replies.

◎

Television shows today can, as the analysis of *Friends* shows, be the subject of serious academic study. The ingenious plays on language in *Buffy the Vampire Slayer*, and the feminist discourse of *Sex and the City*, have both been examined in book form in the last two years. This 'reading' of television is equally apparent in newspapers, which pore over the lives and words of television characters and treat them as no less newsworthy than their non-fictional counterparts. 2004 was a year in which a 'Political Pop Idol' show was mooted a possibility, in which the voting public would choose not a pop star, but rather someone wanting 'to be a leader of the free world'. Meanwhile, the British Mothers' Union voted Marge Simpson of *The Simpsons* the best mother in public life, and viewers of a new teen drama *The O.C.* even believed they were actively directing the plot via their comments on weblogs and chat forums. Messages were posted to the show's creator thanking him for the show's 'shout-out' (a term from hip hop meaning a 'credit') to their suggestions.

◎

This alliance between life and fiction (or, at the very least, carefully choreographed reality) provides language with the perfect opportunity to jump the boundaries between the two. The formula 'I'm a Celebrity . . .' (from the ITV reality TV show *I'm a Celebrity . . . Get Me Out of Here!*) has spawned hundreds of newspaper headlines (most famously *The Sun*'s jibe at former cabinet minister and whistle-blower Clare Short: 'I'm a Liability . . . Get Me Out of Here!') and a vast array of extended uses, just as *Who*

*Wants to be a Millionaire?*'s 'phone a friend' and 'is that your final answer?' have firmly entered our everyday lexicon. When Tony Blair announced an EU referendum U-turn a *Guardian* headline ran 'Yes, no, maybe . . . that's his final answer'.

The influence of television on the words we choose and the way we use them is such that it becomes almost irrelevant if those words are born on the small screen, or simply made available to us because of it. Many forecast the emergence of a language homogenized by mass viewing. Like the Internet, however, television can be the perfect forum for diversity— whether in pronunciation, dialect, or wordplay. We can mix and match the best catchphrases of our TV characters, whether Tony Soprano's 'fuhgeddaboutit', Frasier's 'oh, mama', or Ali G's 'selecta'; in doing so, we introduce colour, comedy, and even a bit of glamour into our own personal 'wordrobes'.

# 24

# Language on Vacation:
## The Art of the Headline

It is clearly important to play with language in order to test its powers . . .
As much as anything else, a pun is language on vacation.
English writer and academic Walter Redfern, *Puns*, 1984.

Headline writing, according to Jim Barger of the *Pittsburgh Post*, is
'one of the last great arts of newspapering. While the rest of the craft
has been downsized . . . the need for a good headline has endured'.
However disposable, the headlines of each period in our recent history
do more than pinpoint the affairs of the moment. They also provide us
with rich examples of wordplay and linguistic creativity. In today's era
of sound-bite journalism and 'infotainment', the twin functions of a
headline, to summarize a story and to seduce the reader into reading
on, are arguably more important now than at any time since the
newspaper began.

There are a number of unwritten rules in headline writing, and almost
all relate to stylistics. One of the most important devices is punning,
previously the preserve of the tabloid newspapers but now also freely
employed by the increasingly less sober broadsheets. *The Gord Giveth* was
a 2004 *Sun* headline following Chancellor Gordon Brown's spring budget,
which used both punning and alliteration—another powerful tool—to
good effect. Clare Short's 'whistle-blowing' on the alleged bugging by
British intelligence of the head of the UN Kofi Anan was, rather inevitably,
headlined *Woman of Mass Destruction* by the *Daily Mail*. Less seriously,
the US news magazine *Science News* carried the wonderful leader *Ancient*

*People Get Dated Down Under* (on new data revealing the period of first migrations to Australia), while *The Sun* back in 2000 borrowed from the *Mary Poppins* song 'supercalifragilisticexpialidocious' with its headline *Super Caley go ballistic, Celtic are atrocious* when lower-league Scottish team Inverness Caledonian Thistle beat Celtic 3–1. Staying with football, the *Guardian* newspaper ran the now famous headline *Queen in Brawl at Palace* when Queens Park Rangers' player Gerry Queen was involved in a punch-up during a match at Crystal Palace. In April 2004, it was *The Sun* again which declared *Zeta does it on the cheapa!*, in rhyming reference to Catherine Zeta-Jones's purchases from the cut-price stores Argos and MFI to furnish a new £1.3 million mansion.

Puns can also draw on more than one theme, and rely on a degree of cultural literacy which, curiously, is rarely seen in headlines beyond British shores. The headline about Gordon Brown above works much better if the reader is aware of the unspoken second part of the allusion from the Bible: 'The Lord gave, and the Lord hath taken away', playing implicitly on the Chancellor's reputation as a 'stealth taxer'. In the same month *The Times* reported on Mars's new, high-fat, chocolate bar, aimed at women, with the headline *Men from Mars give women a fat chance of delight*, and in doing so took a sideways swipe at the best-selling self-help manual *Men are from Mars, Women are from Venus* on its way to a more obvious pun on *fat*.

Newspapers often pile up nouns so that they function essentially as adjectives: the use of so-called 'attributive' nouns or noun modifiers is a defining characteristic of tabloid headlines. The device is a boon to headline writers working within tight space constraints: *Soccer Sex Attack Drama Rushed Out* (*Daily Star*) and numerous versions of 'Shockers' such as *Solvent Test Scheme Shocker* (*Fife Free Press*) and *Kanoute Injury KO Shocker* (*Daily Mirror*) are just a few of the many examples appearing daily.

Rhymes and assonance are equally powerful ingredients in winning headlines. *From Taxman to Axeman* was another reference to Gordon Brown's budget, this time from the right-leaning *Daily Mail*, while the *Mirror's Blunkety Blank* provided a near-perfect example of a headline encompassing almost all of the best stylistic ingredients, playing on the name of Home Secretary David Blunkett and that of the British TV quiz *Blankety Blank*. The headline referred to Blunkett's appearance in the more intellectual quiz *Mastermind*, in which he managed only two points in the general knowledge round. The *Mirror's* great rival *The Sun* later named a competition to guess the asterisked words in David Beckham's alleged adulterous text messages *Play Blankety Becks*.

To contrast modern headlines with those from a century before is revealing. Big-splash headlines were not a feature of newspapers in 1904, and it was not until 1913 that 'banner headlines' of the kind we see today arrived, when they were largely a US phenomenon. Front pages of newspapers such as *The Times* carried birth and death notices and advertisements, with leaders reserved for page 2 onwards. If there was a lack of sensationalism between the pages of the papers, however, the placards of the newspaper-sellers made up the deficit. H. G. Wells, in his *War of the Worlds* (1898), draws on the drama of newsboys' 'read all about it' pitches: 'Fighting at Weybridge! Full description! Repulse of the Martians! London in Danger!'

Today, some parallels with the papers of a century before do remain. With few exceptions, the headlines accompanying major or tragic news stories have remained sober and deliberately uninventive. Exceptions to the rule are all the more striking as a result: the editor of *The Sun*, Rebekah Wade, was chastised for the headline '*Ship, Ship Hooray*', which appeared following the suicide of serial killer Harold Shipman: punning was considered inappropriate even for the man dubbed 'Dr Death'.

Below is a selection of recent successful headlines, some playful, some deadly serious, and all telling examples of the headline writer's art.

## Happy New Fear

Headline in numerous papers, 2 January 2003, reporting on Tony Blair's New Year's message in which he said he could not recall a time 'when Britain was confronted, simultaneously, by such a range of difficult and, in some cases, dangerous problems'.

# Conc Out

The *Sun*, 11 November 2003, announcing the final flight of Concorde on 26 November.

# Porsche Off

*Daily Star*, 7 January 2004, on the 'stunning divorce present' bought by Britney Spears for her ex-husband, after the 22-year-old pop singer wed a childhood friend in a Las Vegas chapel, only to have the marriage annulled fifty hours later.

# Aisle Be Damned

*Washington Post*, 19 March 2004, criticizing George W. Bush's opposition to gay weddings.

# The Sexing Up of Emma

The *Sun*, 3 February 2004, on actress Emma Thompson who wore a 'figure-hugging designer silk gown' to the *Evening Standard* Film Awards. The article also contained the line, 'On the left we leak the secret dossier that shows how Emma was sexed up'.

# Kinky Barbie is Beyond My Ken

*Daily Star*, 16 February 2004, following toy-maker Mattel's announcement that Ken and Barbie are to split after forty-three years.

# Dark Side Over the Moon

The *Sun*, 18 February 2004, after the rock band The Darkness won three Brit awards. The headline is a play on the Pink Floyd album, *The Dark Side of the Moon*.

# Dosh and Pecs

The *Sun*, 21 February 2004, adapting the nicknames of David and Victoria ('Posh Spice') Beckham to fit two stars on the TV reality show *I'm a Celebrity . . . Get Me Out of Here!*, Jordan and Peter Andre. The article related how 'jungle lovers Jordan and Peter Andre will earn £5 million in their first year as a showbiz couple'.

## A Very British Excuse

The *Express*, 9 March 2004, on the disappearance of the Mars probe 'Beagle 2', due to land on Christmas Day 2003, which was blamed on the 'wrong kind of dust' and on the weather. Both excuses have been notorious in Britain since British Rail blamed train disruptions on 'the wrong kind of leaves' on the line. The line is also a play on the title of the TV drama series *A Very British Coup*.

## It's A Jor Dropper

The *Sun*, 15 March 2004, on former glamour model Jordan. The first paragraph of the article goes on 'Here's the latest chapter in the "take me seriously" life of Jordan, as she shows off her mighty cleavage'.

## Our September 11th—A Day of Infamy

The Spanish newspaper *El Mundo* on 12 March 2004, following the terrorist bombs in Madrid. The headline echoes Franklin Roosevelt's description of Pearl Harbor as 'a day that will live in infamy'.

## It's All Over—The Fat Bloke's Sung

*The Guardian*, 15 March 2004, on Pavarotti's announcement that his performance in *Tosca* in New York was to be his last in a staged opera (and with allusion to the phrase 'it's not over until the fat lady sings').

## Zombies Drive Jesus From Top of Box Office

Music channel MTV, February 2004, on the overtaking of Mel Gibson's film *The Passion of the Christ* by the remake of *The Dawn of the Dead* as the biggest box-office draw.

## Martha Stewart: Spiffing Up the Joint

The *Seattle Post-Intelligencer*, 19 March 2004, on the jail sentence given to domestic doyenne Martha Stewart for unlawful share trading.

## It Fakes a Village

Title of a negative review in the *New York Times*, 19 March 2004, of Lars von Trier's film *Dogville*, set in a small Colorado town. The headline plays on the title of Hillary Clinton's book *It Takes A Village* (to raise a child).

## More Than One Way To Skin a Copycat

*Wired* magazine, 2 April 2004, on new software which can detect plagiarism.

## Posh and Tex. Is It All Over?

Front-cover headline of the satirical magazine *Private Eye*, April 2004, showing a picture of Tony Blair and George Bush, and in the week of blanket coverage of David Beckham's alleged adulterous affairs.

## Apocalypse Now?

The *Sunday Times*, 11 April 2004, on post-war anarchy in Iraq and playing on the film of the same title.

## Mor . . . Gone! It's all gone Piers shaped

A spoof headline from the *Daily Mirror* accompanying a *Sunday Times* article, 16 May 2004, detailing the sacking of the *Mirror's* editor Piers Morgan for publishing a series of photographs purporting to show the torture of Iraqi prisoners by British troops. One of the *Mirror's* earlier headlines had been the one-word **Vile**; on the day after Morgan's departure, it ran the line **Sorry: We Were Hoaxed**.

## You Swiss Banker

*The Sun*, 25 June 2004, after England was knocked out of the Euro 2004 football tournament. Swiss referee Urs Meier diallowed a last-minute goal, which would have taken the English team into the semi finals.

## Football's Coming Homer

*The Guardian*, 5 July 2004, after Greece won Euro 2004. The odds on a Greek victory stood at 100/1 at the start of the tournament.

## What the Butler Saw

The online publication *Spiked*, 14 July 2004, on the findings of Lord Butler's report investigating the accuracy of intelligence concerning Iraq's weapons of mass destruction. The headline used the title of Joe Orton's 1969 play; a 'what the butler saw' was a seaside coin-in-the-slot machine which played short motion pictures of women undressing. The phrase became a byword for shameful secrets or voyeurism.

## Vice is Right

*The Sun*, 17 July 2004, on government proposals to legalize prostitution in Britain. The headline plays on the name of the game-show *The Price is Right*.

# A century before

## The Mission to Tibet. The Retreat of the Natives

*The Times*, 5 April 1904. In 1904 British forces invaded Tibet under Francis Younghusband with a brief to establish and protect British interests amid ongoing suspicion of Russian intentions. After a series of bloody conflicts, in which many Tibetans died, an agreement was reached between Younghusband and the Tibetan government.

## Death of Mr Whitaker Wright

*The Times*, 28 January 1904. J. Whitaker Wright, a financier and speculative promoter of gold mines in Western Australia, was convicted of fraud following the spectacular collapse of his empire. The celebrated case of King vs. Whitaker Wright came to trial in 1904; Whitaker Wright committed suicide shortly after a guilty verdict.

## Through the Panama Canal

*The Times*, 24 May 1904. Work on the Panama Canal began in earnest in 1904, led by the US and Theodore Roosevelt, who had abetted a revolution by the Panamanians in order to secure construction through the

Colombian state. Roosevelt would later boast about the signal event of his presidency by proclaiming 'I took Panama'.

# Denmark agog over whipping-post

*Daily Review*, 3 November 1904, on reported Danish plans to reintroduce whipping posts for thugs.

# The Outrage By the Baltic Fleet. Severe Foreign Comments.

*The Times*, 25 October 1904. The headline is in reference to the 'Dogger Bank' incident, when the Russian Baltic Fleet mistook a Swedish ship for a Japanese torpedo boat during the Russo-Japanese war. Later that night the Russian fleet thought it was again under attack by the Japanese, and opened fire on what proved to be British trawlers in the North Sea off Dogger Bank, sinking one, *The Crane*. Their actions nearly precipitated a European war.

# Democrats Buried Deep

*Nashua (Iowa) Reporter*, on the day after Theodore Roosevelt was re-elected President on 10 November 1904 by the largest margin in US history, receiving over 2 million more votes than Alton Parker. It was his first time of election in his own right, having been vice-president when McKinley was assassinated in 1901.

# 25

# A Word a Year:
## 1904–2004

Very few words are coined in isolation. Each neologism holds a clue, however faint, of the time in which it was created. The following choice of a single word from each of the last hundred years is inevitably subjective, since hundreds of new words are being created at any one time. Nonetheless, collectively these words give a distinct picture of the shifting preoccupations of the 20th century and the early years of the 21st.

**1904  hip**
    (as in smart, or stylish)

**1905  whizzo**
    (an interjection expressing delight)

**1906  teddy bear**
    (named in humorous allusion to the US President Theodore (Teddy) Roosevelt)

**1907  egghead**
    (an intellectual or 'highbrow')

**1908  realpolitik**
    (from the German meaning 'practical politics', i.e. politics determined by practical rather than ideological considerations)

**1909 tiddly-om-pom-pom**
(representing the sound of brass-band or similar music. The *OED*'s
first citation is from the now traditional British song *I do like to be
beside the seaside*)

**1910 sacred cow**
(used at this time as a journalistic term, meaning a person not to
be criticized, or copy not to be cut)

**1911 gene**

**1912 blues**

**1913 celeb**

**1914 cheerio**

**1915 civvy street**
(the return to civilian life was known as 'going back to civvy street')

**1916 U-boat**

**1917 tailspin**
(the downward movement of an aircraft in which the tail spirals)

**1918 ceasefire**

**1919 ad-lib**

**1920 demob**
(short for 'demobilize', moving an armed force onto a peace
footing)

**1921 pop**
(as in 'pop song')

**1922 wizard**
(very good)

**1923 hem-line**

**1924 lumpenproletariat**
(a term applied by Karl Marx to the lowest and most degraded
section of the proletariat, who make no contribution to the
workers' cause)

**1925 avant garde**

**1926 kitsch**

**1927 sudden death**
(in sport, a toss or period of extra time to bring a game to a
sudden, decisive conclusion)

**1928 Big Apple**
(New York City)

**1929 sex**
(i.e. as a shortening of 'sexual intercourse')

**1930 drive-in**

**1931 Mickey Mouse**
(as an adjective meaning 'inauthentic', or 'worthless')

**1932 bagel**

**1933 dumb down**

**1934 pesticide**

**1935 racism**

**1936 spliff**

**1937 dunk**
(in basketball, to push the ball down through the basket)

**1938 cheeseburger**

**1939 Blitzkrieg**
(German for 'lightning war', i.e. a quick and decisive war)

**1940 Molotov cocktail**
(a makeshift incendiary device for throwing by hand, consisting of a bottle or other breakable container filled with flammable liquid)

**1941 snafu**
(an acronym for 'situation normal, all fouled (or fucked) up'. The expression was meant to convey a soldier's resigned acceptance of the disorder of war and the ineptitude of his superiors)

**1942 buzz**
(a sense of excitement)

**1943 pissed off**

**1944 DNA**

**1945 mobile phone**

**1946 megabucks**

**1947 Wonderbra**

**1948 cool**

**1949 Big Brother**
(an apparently benevolent, but ruthlessly omnipotent, state authority. The term was coined by George Orwell in his novel *1984*)

**1950 brainwashing**

**1951 fast food**

**1952 Generation X**
(a lost, disillusioned generation)

**1953 hippy**

**1954 non-U**
(a British term indicating a lower social status, especially of social or linguistic behaviour. 'U' behaviour described the accepted conventions of the upper class. Nancy Mitford's coining of the terms in her essay *Noblesse Oblige* prompted a national debate about English snobbery)

**1955 boogie**
(as a verb)

**1956 sexy**
(as an adjective meaning 'interesting')

**1957 psychedelic**

**1958 beatnik**
(one of the 'beat generation', who adopted unconventional fashion and behaviour as a form of self-expression and social protest)

**1959 cruise missile**

**1960 cyborg**
(an integrated man-machine)

**1961 awesome**
(in a general sense meaning 'amazing')

**1962 bossa nova**
(a style of Brazilian music related to the samba)

**1963 peacenik**
(a member of a pacifist movement, and usually also a hippy)

**1964 byte**

**1965 miniskirt**

**1966 acid**
(the hallucinogenic drug LSD)

**1967 love-in**

**1968 It-girl**
(a girl who is sexually alluring. Today's additional implications
of a socialite lifestyle are relatively new)

**1969 microchip**

**1970 hypermarket**

**1971 green**
(concerned with protecting the environment)

**1972 Watergate**

**1973 F-word**

**1974 punk**

**1975 detox**

**1976 Trekkie**
(a committed fan of the TV series *Star Trek*)

**1977 naff all**
(British, meaning 'nothing at all' and a euphemism for 'fuck all')

**1978 trainers**

**1979 karaoke**

**1980 power dressing**

**1981 toy-boy**

**1982 hip-hop**

**1983 beatbox**
(an electronic drum machine)

**1984 double-click**
(as a verb)

**1985 OK yah**
(a British expression parodying upper-middle class speech, originally that of 'Sloane Rangers')

**1986 mobile**
(for 'mobile phone')

**1987 virtual reality**

**1988 gangsta**
(a gangster, particularly used in rap lyrics)

**1989 latte**

**1990 applet**
(a small application programme on a computer)

**1991 hot-desking**
(allocating or using desks on a temporary basis to save resources)

**1992 URL**
(abbreviation for 'universal resource locator', the address of a World Wide Web page)

**1993 have it large**
(to enjoy something to the full)

**1994 Botox**

**1995 kitten heels**

**1996 ghetto fabulous**
(ostentatiously fashionable and expensive)

**1997 dot-commer**
(someone who conducts their business on the internet)

**1998 text message**

**1999 google**
(as a verb, to use the Google search engine)

**2000 bling bling**
(see pages 70–71)

**2001 9/11**

**2002 axis of evil**

**2003 sex up**

**2004 chav**
(a group of people pejoratively described as delinquents and
members of an underclass. See pages 142–143)